Govardhan Gabbi is a Punjabi writer, who was born in 1966 in Pathankot, Punjab, and presently lives in Chandigarh. A former member of the Advisory Council (Punjabi) Sahitya Akademi, New Delhi, he has written two books of poetry, *Dil Wali Fatadi* (2002) and *Ateet De Sirnavein* (2005), three books of short stories *Gurdakhana* (2009), *Bharamjaal* (2012), and *Tin Tiye Satt* (2017), and a novel, *Puran Katha* (2015), among other writings. He writes regular columns for many Punjabi daily newspapers and literary magazines.

PURAN GAATHA

A PARTITION SAGA

GOVARDHAN GABBI

Translated By
Dr Rajinder Singh

Om Books International

First published in 2024 by

Om Books International

Corporate & Editorial Office
A-12, Sector 64, Noida 201 301
Uttar Pradesh, India
Phone: +91 120 477 4100
Email: editorial@ombooks.com
Website: www.ombooksinternational.com

Sales Office
107, Ansari Road, Darya Ganj,
New Delhi 110 002, India
Phone: +91 11 4000 9000
Email: sales@ombooks.com
Website: www.ombooks.com

ISBN: 978-93-5376-853-9

Printed in India

10 9 8 7 6 5 4 3 2 1

Dedicated to my mother Bachno Devi, whose unconditional love empowered my father to overcome every adversity

One

Though it is not certain, the year of my birth, as recorded in official documents and based on what my mother and Chacha used to tell me, is 1936. It could have been a year earlier or later. And the month and date may also be slightly off. It is pointless to guess the time of my birth, but we can believe that it was the night of 6 or 7 January. I can say this because whenever I asked my mother about the time of my birth, she would say, 'What can I tell you, Puran! When you were born, it was so cold our teeth would chatter. Girls and boys used to come begging for treats, so Lohri must have been approaching. Oh yes, another thing—I had given up breast-feeding Charan just a month earlier. The wretched one was two or two and a half years old. I don't remember the year, but you were born ten or eleven years before the Partition. I don't remember much else, my dear son.'

I am quite certain of the village I was born in because while times may change, places do not. Of course, the features of a place do change. Oceans turn into mountains and mountains become oceans. Barren lands turn fertile, and fertile lands turn into deserts. Where there was wilderness once, modern cities develop in no time. Change is the law of nature. Man should also change, otherwise the development of human beings would stop. With the stoppage of development, there would be stagnation, and stagnation is the other name of death.

I was born in a small village, Khohli, in Block Shakargarh, District Gurdaspur, in the province of Punjab, which is in modern-day Pakistan. When I speak of Pakistan today, I don't know why, but my heart misses a few beats. I am unable to control my tears. Thinking of the place of my birth, my heart weeps. Scenes from the time I spent there appear before my eyes like a movie. I think of the ways in which times change. Your own become othered, and sometimes others become your own forever. Time is so very powerful. Indeed, time is the most powerful. It has never been a slave to anyone. Nor will it ever be.

Our parents were not only poor, but they were also illiterate. Our family was large. In those days, having a large family was favoured. The thinking was that the more children one had, the more hands there would be to work, and with more hands, income too would be all the more. Hunger always influences one's thinking. Perhaps that is why I did not see the inside of a school, but that was not the only reason why I remained uneducated. The main reason was the noise about the Partition of India.

There was a hue and cry all around. Stabbings and killings were reported daily. Hindus were being killed. Muslims too were being done to death. Sikhs were being beheaded. As always, daughters and sisters, no matter what their faith, were being raped and molested.

As is customary, the representatives of the political parties were, as the saying goes, 'baking their loaves on the pyre of humanity'. Public meetings were held everywhere by the parties—large gatherings, speeches, processions—but no one had a meaningful solution; neither the British nor the political leaders, whether Nehru, Gandhi or Jinnah. In fact, the British wanted to use any means possible to divide the country before they left.

Ultimately, they succeeded in dividing our country into two nations.

The people were panic-stricken. If a person left home in the morning, the eyes of the members of the family remained fixed on the entrance of the house till they returned.

In such an atmosphere, my not going to school was of little consequence. Also, my parents did not understand the importance of educating children; or perhaps they did not want to understand. Or perhaps another reason was that they could not afford to educate all their children.

Therefore, like many other children, I had no experience of attending school.

I watched my companions from a distance as they went to school. I cursed my fate.

'I too want to go to school, Mother, like brother Punjab Das and Fazlu. Enrol me too,' I would request my mother.

'My dear son, we are very hard up this year, but next year, I will certainly send you to school,' my mother would say to me every year.

She did try to send me every year, but the times and the prevailing conditions prevented her from succeeding. Every year, I saw my dream shattered and suffered disappointment. This dream was not fulfilled till the end.

Ultimately, on 15 August 1947, India attained independence, but it was partitioned into two nations. Our leaders suffered defeat, and the British succeeded in their mission.

The people of the country were both happy and sad. It was a strange combination of joy and sorrow. They were happy because freedom had been attained but sad because the country had been partitioned. Two nations had emerged. It was as if on the one hand, your father had departed for his heavenly abode, but on the other, you had been blessed with a son on the same day.

A new country, Pakistan, was born after truncating India and appeared on the world map.

On the one hand, celebrations were underway, on the other, killing and looting were taking place.

Lakhs of people were killed during the Partition riots: displaced, rendered homeless and dishonoured. Centuries-old ties were shredded in a moment. Brothers turned into enemies—thirsty for one another's blood. It took no time to turn friendships into enmity. It seemed as if God had hidden Himself or that He did not want to witness the naked dance of man's brutality. But the dance, which had to take place, did take place. The streams of blood, which had to flow, did flow. The hatred, which had to spread, did spread. The distances, the gulfs and the chasms in the people's minds did get created.

A strange void had been produced. Terrible. Painful. One that could never be filled. One that had to fester. One that is still festering and shall keep festering till the end of time.

It appeared as though humanity were crossing over from that side to this side and from this side to that side. Fighting and killing and getting killed. Thirsty for one another's blood. Some thirsts can be quenched with water, but some are not quenched even by drinking blood.

On the other hand, our family was not ready to believe that they would have to leave the village of their ancestors.

'Like the din and noise of the past, this noise too will die down sooner or later...We need not worry too much...Don't pay much heed to these rumours; they are such baseless things...Pay heed to your work; don't waste your time on such trifles,' Chacha would say, arguing with those who counselled him to leave for India.

Perhaps our family's thinking and reasoning were so due to their being uneducated and having no insight into political affairs. Or perhaps it was their love for their place of birth that compelled them to not accept ground reality. But reality is always reality. If a pigeon shuts its eyes at the sight of a cat and thinks the cat has gone away, then it is the pigeon's foolishness. That is what our family was doing.

The inevitable happened. Political leaders and the people at large fell victim to the clever games of the white man.

A country that had fought against the British for freedom for two hundred years was divided on attainment of that freedom.

That division was both of the land and in people's hearts. The ill-fated Punjab had to bear the brunt of the Partition. The knife of division, tearing apart the chest of the earth, shed so much blood that many centuries will not be enough to heal the wounds.

Some wounds are beyond healing and turn into cancer with the passage of time. Doctors are still unable to treat cancer fully.

Everything happened in a few days' time. Two countries came into being. Two flags came up. Two nations emerged. Separate.

On the other hand, our family wanted to remain in their village. They never accepted the fact that there would be two countries, that India would be divided. But reality did not change to conform to their thinking. Could the partition of the country be reversed? No, the country had been divided.

'How can we leave our village? Jinnah has declared, "Yours is a separate country; ours is separate. Your God is different from our Allah." But I will not leave the land of my ancestors, my country. Why should I leave my house, my village, the centuries-old memories, our brotherhood, our association? How can I tell my bosom friend Fazlu that I can no longer live with him because I am not a Muslim? I will have to cross over to the other side, to the Hindus' side, because I am a Hindu. Why should I suffer loss at the insistence of these political leaders? I don't believe their speeches. I will not go anywhere, leaving my own home and hearth. Why should I become a refugee in my own land?' Chacha continued to argue with others.

Many families were leaving, but our family stuck to its rigid stand.

They had made up their mind to not leave Pakistan.

Forgetting everything, we got busy with our daily routine. We had taken the Partition as a temporary edict, one that could be taken back at any time by the two countries, but we did not know that water that has flowed under a bridge does not come back. And even if it does return, it is in a different form.

Our mother, whom all of us brothers and sisters called Bebe, was named Mangla Devi, and our father, whom we all called Chacha, was named Keshav Ram.

My eldest sister, Shanti Devi, and the brother younger than her, Babu Ram, had been married before the Partition.

I had three older brothers. The eldest was Babu Ram. The next was Punjab Das, and then was Charan

Das, and then I, the youngest, Puran Chand, and my younger sister was Bhano Devi.

In 1947, my eldest sister was about twenty-two or twenty-three years old.

My father's elder brother, whom we called Taya, and our family did contract farming in the adjoining village, Azizpur. Taya also had five sons and two daughters. All of them were also illiterate.

Chacha did send Babu Ram and Punjab Das to school. Babu Ram could not study, but at the time of the Partition, Punjab Das had passed the ninth class. Before he could begin the tenth class, the disturbances surrounding the Partition had initiated.

When he was a child, Babu Ram once slipped and fell out of a tree he had climbed. His chin was badly hurt. He was operated upon at General Hospital in Lahore. The doctors had to remove the fractured part of the bone but were able to save the jawbone. His chin caved inwards because of the injury, causing a dent.

It took more than six months for him to recover.

Because of his dented chin, it was difficult to find a matrimonial alliance for him. For a long time, no girl could be found who was willing to be married to him, but ultimately, he was married.

Chacha ran a small shop in the village.

Charan and I would take the cattle out to graze and cut grass.

Ours was not a big village. A monsoon stream passed through the middle, dividing the village into two parts: the small quarter and the big quarter. Everyone referred to the village by these names. We lived in the big quarter.

In the big quarter, there were about twenty houses belonging to Katal Rajputs, five houses to us Ariyans, four to Muslim peasants, two to the bards, and one each to the pundits and water carriers.

In the small quarter were five houses each of Rajputs and Mahashas, and two each of Julahas and carpenters. In all, there were about fifty to fifty-five houses in the entire village. In the dry season, the monsoon streambed served the purpose of a ground. Village children and grown-up boys and girls would play there. There was also a temple and a large banyan tree nearby. Those who came to the temple to pay obeisance enjoyed sitting in the shade of the tree. The elders in the village played cards under this tree. A big wrestling fair was held annually in this ground. Wrestlers from far and near came to compete in the wrestling matches. There was a river flowing to the east of the village. It was known as Karir. The river would flood during the rains. The hissing waters were quite frightening at night. There were two grinding mills also, driven by bullocks, in the big divide. People from neighbouring villages would go there to have their wheat and maize ground.

The village land was rain-fed and uneven, full of hollows and dunes. If the monsoon was good, the crops were also good; otherwise, the land remained barren.

There was a big village, Lesar, to the south of our village. The post office for Khohli village was located there.

Shakargarh was six miles from our village.

All the villagers lived in harmony and amity. They joined in one another's joys and sorrows. Very few caste-based or communal clashes took place. All of them united against any adversity.

One day, I was walking with my grandmother towards the fields. She held on her head with one hand a small basket containing foodstuffs, and in the other hand, she held a water jug. I was walking along, stomping on the ground. Now, marching on the raised edges of the fields, we had with us breakfast for the members of our family working in the fields.

Suddenly, someone hit or frightened a small pup, and it ran towards us, bumping into my grandmother's legs. She slipped and fell, fracturing her hip bone.

It could not be set right till her death. She had to endure very difficult times after that.

The noise about the Partition grew louder with every passing day. Many people were migrating.

My uncle had left Azizpur and come to Khohli.

Taya's and our families were living in the same house.

Both the families had their own rooms, but the courtyard was common.

Those who considered themselves wise had moved to India as soon as the disturbances had started. There were some who had taken their livestock and other belongings to Jammu State but had continued to stay in the village. They hoped the unrest would be short-lived, and they would be able to bring their belongings back. Chacha did neither. He was hopeful that the Partition would never take place.

'Up till now, we have seen members of a family separating or a family being divided. Can a country ever be divided? People are talking rot. All these are mere rumours, just din and noise…Everything will be all right in a few days,' Chacha would reason not only with the members of the family but with others as well.

Some people believed Chacha. They were ready to do as he counselled.

Chacha had refused to migrate to India. Many people in the adjoining villages also made up their mind not to leave.

Killings had started in the villages. The massacre of humanity was at its peak.

The Muslims, who were coming this side from India, were occupying the houses vacated by the Hindus who had left. The Sikhs and Hindus who had gone from this side had begun to occupy the houses left behind by the Muslims.

Those who were coming from India to Pakistan were saying that the Muslims were being massacred in India. The Hindus and Sikhs were picking up Muslims and killing them. They were sending trains full of migrants to this side. The same was happening on this side. Trains full of dead bodies of Sikhs and Hindus went to India. The situation was horrible. There was panic and destruction all around.

Hearing this, many Muslims in the neighbouring villages had begun to enter our villages in bands. Whenever they heard of Sikhs and Hindus still living there, fifteen or twenty of them would come together and wherever they found a Hindu or a Sikh, they would kill them. They took their young daughters and wives with them.

Both of our families remained in hiding by day in the houses of our Muslim brethren. We passed our days in this way. Panicked, like children.

Pakistan had been created five or six months earlier.

The governments of the two countries had sealed their borders. The migration had stopped.

All the members of our families believed that they would not have to leave their village.

After a few days, the governments of India and Pakistan began to set up refugee camps under the supervision of the army. The Hindus left in Pakistan and the Muslims left in India were being sent to India and Pakistan respectively through these camps.

The military men went to the villages and set up camps. Those who came to know of them migrated through these camps. This continued for about two weeks.

Unfortunately, no military man came to our village, nor did anyone come to know about a camp. Almost all the Hindus of the neighbouring fifteen to twenty villages had gone to India through these camps, except two or three families in our village.

After some days, Pakistan invaded Jammu State.

Tension prevailed all the more. Many types of news started coming in. Fear and panic filled the minds of everyone.

Pakistani military vehicles passed through our villages. There were armed civilian Pathans with them as well. If those Pathans came to know about the presence of Hindus or Sikhs anywhere, they robbed them.

They were not afraid of anything. Looting and arson were everywhere.

One day, we too were spotted by the Pathans.

It was about 5 p.m. I was playing ball with my mates outside our house. A Muslim youth approached our house with eight or nine armed Pathans. After showing them our place, he slipped away. The Pathans entered our house. They searched it thoroughly. Whatever jewellery and cash had been hidden, the Pathans carried away with them. When the householders opposed them, they thrashed everyone.

'If you are seen in this village when we return, you will not be safe. Pick up your belongings and get away from here,' the Pathans said and left.

We were already terrified. This threat made us panic more. We feared we'd lose our lives if they returned to the village. After this, none of us slept in the house but near a sugarcane crusher in the village.

We somehow made it through that night, but how and where we would spend the nights to come was eating all of us up. We stared at one another with fearful eyes, but no one knew what to do.

At daybreak, we returned home, cooked a meal and filled our bellies.

All the members of the remaining Hindu families got together to discuss the future course of action.

Panic had entered our minds, and when panic occupies the mind, the brain becomes sick and oftentimes inactive. Just dead. The members of our families were in that condition.

After a long discussion, it was decided that we would cross the border of Jammu State that night. This border was closer to the Indian border. Travelling with very young children was going to be an uphill task. My grandmother, with her fractured hip bone, had with her another old lady who lived with us. She was the mother-in-law of my elder sister, Shanti Devi. Her family had left her with us and had crossed the border themselves. She could walk but not much. Being very old, she tired easily.

Firstly, as we had with us very young children and two old women, Chacha and the others were not able to muster the courage to leave. Secondly, we had to leave stealthily. Though I was a child, I could well understand the calamity that had befallen the family. Even though I wished to, I could do nothing.

When the old ladies came to know that the family would not be able to cross the border because of them, both folded their hands before Chacha.

'Son, we have seen enough of life. What is the point of taking us across the border? We were born on this side, and we wish to die on this side. We do not want to suffer at this age. Leave us here and go across the border with the other members of the family.'

Tears permeated the eyes of the two women as my grandmother said these words.

Chacha's eyes were also teary. He kept quiet for some time.

Then he proposed that he would stay on with his old mother and the other old lady. The other members of the family could cross the border. When the unrest eased, they would get to India with the help of the state government or the Indian government.

Initially, no one agreed to this plan, but later on, the family began to prepare to carry out the proposal made by Chacha.

A Muslim neighbour from our village was asked to accompany us to the border as he was familiar with the terrain. His company was also necessary to protect us against attacks on the way.

At night, without informing our neighbours, all of us gathered a few of our belongings and put the bundles on our heads.

Both the old women and Chacha saw us off.

The members of the families set out to cross the border, led by the Muslim man from our village.

It was a very cold winter's night.

We had gone a little beyond the border of the village when evil entered our guide's mind. The sword he had held to protect us, he now raised against us. Everyone loves their life.

My brothers tried to bring him round but our escort, blinded by greed, became our sworn enemy. Threatening us with his sword, he took our jewellery and cash and other expensive items. Abusing our mothers and sisters, he returned to the village.

When one's protector turns into an enemy, what can one do?

Everyone sat down, stunned and lost. Should we proceed or return, we could not decide. We could not talk loudly because of the fear of being caught.

Ultimately, we decided that going back would be of no avail and therefore we should continue.

Having lost almost everything, the group proceeded.

Towards an unknown destination.

Without knowing the way.

We were in all twenty or twenty-five persons.

The severe cold was unbearable. Then the sky became cloudy. A light drizzle began.

We moved in a single file on the footpath.

It was a pitch-dark, cold night. Death loomed large. There was the constant fear of being spotted by the enemy. No one had seen the route to the border before. We had abandoned the main path because we feared being caught. We were walking across the monsoon streambed towards Jammu. Quiet, panicked and fearful. Fear of being killed. Fear of being caught. We dared not talk to one another.

As we moved on, we got separated from one another.

A few of us took to a footpath and others got on another path.

The one good thing was that all the members of my family remained together; Taya's elder son Rasalo was also with our group. He was of the same age as my elder brother Babu Ram. There were two or three girls and some children in the group. All the children held their elders' hands. The night was so dark that one could not see even one's own hand. The rain had created more trouble for us. Our clothes had gotten wet. It was bitingly cold. We were in the midst of desolate forest land. The fear of death haunted us. We had no idea of the right way. The sounds of wild animals, insects and crickets were frightening. All of us were moving towards an unseen destination.

We kept walking through the night but where we were, we did not know.

When cocks began to crow at about 4 a.m., some visibility returned.

The rain had also ceased.

After some time, we realized that we were moving in the right direction.

Suddenly, we spotted some houses.

Babu Ram was familiar with this village. It was Khaira Gujran village. It was about one and a half miles away from the border.

We met a watchman on the outskirts of the village.

All of us had turned blue because of the severe cold. Our teeth were chattering.

Babu Ram, who smoked the hookah, asked the watchman to fetch some coal blocks for him. He obliged and soon returned from the village, accompanied by four or five Gujjar men.

Babu Ram lit his hookah. The Gujjars started a bonfire. In the process of talking, Babu Ram told them that we were planning to cross the border.

As soon as he disclosed this, the Gujjars turned hostile. They ordered us not to stir from the bonfire.

All our efforts to escape had proved futile.

At daybreak, they informed the military stationed in the next village about us.

There were four or five young girls and a few women in our group.

The Gujjars' intentions turned dishonourable. They decided to hand over one of our men to the army and hide the rest of us. The girls and women would be kept, and the others would be helped to cross or be killed.

They were discussing all this behind our backs, but I overheard them as I was standing with their children. Dismissing me as a mere child, they continued to deliberate.

After some time, they approached the family.

'Don't worry. You are like our brothers. We will help you cross the border at night so the army does not spot you. Till then, let's do this—your women should get busy working with our women so that no one suspects anything, and the menfolk can come with us to work outside.'

As they talked, saliva dripped from their lips.

They had changed colours like a chameleon.

The members of our family agreed to their suggestion.

They believed that the Gujjars were sincere, but I had learnt their true intentions. Being a child, I accompanied Bebe to their house. Playing with their children, I again overheard the Gujjars. They were discussing the same thing as earlier. When I heard them for the second time, I got scared.

Finding an opportunity, I conveyed their plan to my brothers, but they would not believe me. Rather, they chided me for being foolish. I was talking nonsense. Taking me for a mere child, they paid no heed to what I had told them, but the fear of death had entered my mind.

What should be done?

My family was not heeding me.

I got terribly upset.

To save my life, I slipped out of the house.

I went out of the village. I could see some hills to the east.

Though a child, I guessed that the border would be towards the hills.

And towards the hills, I began to march.

It was afternoon. I had walked just half a mile when I heard voices. I looked back and saw that four or five Gujjar boys were running towards me.

On the pretext of easing myself, I sat down behind a bush.

It was a good way of hiding my intention.

They drew closer and stopped but said nothing.

After some time, I was back with my family.

What had transpired outside, I did not share with anyone.

Bebe and the other members of the family were still discussing the future course of action with the Gujjars. The plan was that when the military men arrived, the Gujjars would say that they had held only one person. They persuaded Rasalo to play the part of the captured person. They also told him that the army would help him get to Jammu State.

Meanwhile, the others should remain in hiding so that they could be helped to cross over at night.

I knew the evil-mindedness of these Gujjars who appeared to be so very well meaning, but our family was convinced about their charitable intentions. They made Rasalo accept the story that he was going to cross over all alone and was being held.

Everyone was asked to act according to the plan.

In the evening, a military vehicle stopped outside the village.

The military men sent word to the Gujjars that the persons held by them at night should be brought to the crossing.

All of us hid in the Gujjars' house.

The Gujjars took Rasalo with them to the military men at the crossing.

There, Rasalo found that his father Ranjhu and others in the family were already with them. They were serving them tea and refreshments.

Later on, he found out that his family had been held in some other village. The military men planned to take everyone they had found heading for the border, including Rasalo and his family, to their cantonment in the same vehicle.

The Gujjars presented Rasalo before a military officer.

Rasalo spotted his father and other members of the family sitting at a distance. He was stunned. But the Gujjars had told him to say something else.

His father and others of the family approached him.

At the first opportunity, Rasalo whispered in his father's ear, requesting him to keep quiet.

Rasalo and his father resembled each other very much.

The military officer was a smart man. He looked at Rasalo and then at his father. He felt that they appeared to be father and son.

'Do you know this elder one sitting here?' he asked Rasalo.

'No, sir, I do not know him.' Rasalo looked at his father fearfully and mustered the courage to reply.

His tone and manner increased the military officer's suspicion.

'Tell me, old man, is this boy speaking the truth? Is he not related to you in any way?'

What could Taya do? He too refused to recognize him, as Rasalo had told him to.

The military officer was not convinced with their replies. Things looked suspicious to him. He became furious. He pulled out his gun and aimed it at Rasalo.

'All right, Baba, if he is not related to you, I am going to shoot him,' said the officer.

Before Ranjhu could say anything, his wife—that is Rasalo's mother—shrieked loudly.

She started crying bitterly and blurted out the truth.

She begged the military officer not to kill her son.

'You can shoot me, sir. But the other members of our family, whom these Gujjars have hidden, should be brought here...you must spare their lives...'

Seeing his mother crying and begging, Rasalo too took courage and opened his mouth to say something.

Then he and his mother clasped each other and kept crying.

The military officer was a kind-hearted person.

He was furious with the Gujjars. He and his men thrashed the Gujjars thoroughly.

The Gujjars begged the officer to forgive them and were let off.

The officer sent two men with the Gujjars to bring back the other members of our larger family.

All the members of the two families were reunited. Everyone cried and embraced one another.

The military men took all of us to the cantonment in their vehicles.

We were asked to stay in a vacant house in Kharali village. They permitted us to beg for flour from the village and cook our food.

Hatred had spread so very widely during those days that Hindus did not partake of food in Muslim houses and Muslims did likewise.

The elders made slings out of sheets tied to my and my brother Charan's waists and shoulders and sent us to beg for flour and pulses.

I got flour in my sling and Charan Das received pulses.

We returned after collecting about five kilos of flour and pulses.

We cooked our meal and spent the night in the village.

The military men sent us word early the next morning to appear in their office at 9 a.m.

When we got there, they told us that we had to go to Shakargarh.

There, the tehsildar would tell us what to do.

We carried our belongings on our heads and marched towards Shakargarh.

Two military havildars accompanied us, riding their horses. They led us, and we followed them.

We had spent a sleepless night and were hungry, but we had to walk for four or five hours. Shakargarh was quite far away. The children were crying, their empty stomachs wreaking havoc.

The havildars took pity on us. They told us to rest as we reached the next village on the way.

Humanity had not yet died. In the village, the members of a Muslim family showed kindness to us. They cooked food and fed us.

After eating our meal, we went to sleep.

Meanwhile, the havildars went and met the tehsildar.

He ordered us to return to the cantonment.

We returned late that night.

We cooked our food and spent the night in the same house as before.

In the morning, we were ordered to return to our own village.

Meanwhile, the military had called the headman of our village, the *nambardar*. We were handed over to him.

We walked back and reached our village in the evening.

Chacha and the old ladies were happy to receive us. They were relieved to see us safe and sound, but sad that we were not able to cross the border.

After a fierce struggle for three days, we had returned to our own home.

At daybreak, everyone got busy with their usual work.

The old routine was resumed.

There was an unease that occupied our minds. It was troubling us. Many thoughts arose in our minds and then died down, leaving us worried and disturbed.

We did not want to continue living in the village, which now appeared to be a strange place. But we had no choice.

Whenever we saw the Muslim man who had looted us, we felt stunned, but we could do nothing.

Now our own country had become 'othered'. Our own people seemed to be 'others'. It takes no time for the environment to change.

We had begun to view every Muslim brother with suspicion.

Considering all things, we did not want to live in our village, Khohli, which had turned hostile.

One day, Chacha and Babu Ram went to the nearby village of Azizpur, where Taya used to farm land belonging to Muslim choudhries on a contract basis. When Taya had worked there, Chacha would go to Azizpur to meet him. So the choudhries knew Chacha as well. They were good people. Chacha related his tale of woe to them. He told them that he had to live by farming and therefore wanted to lease land from them. The choudhries also needed farmers, and so they agreed. Chacha also told them that as soon as we got an opportunity, the family would leave for India.

The choudhries promised to arrange for two or three bullock carts so that we could transport our belongings from Khohli to Azizpur.

Chacha and Babu Ram returned to our village.

The family members got together in the evening to discuss the future.

In the morning, we prepared to leave Khohli to go to Azizpur.

The bullock carts arrived by ten.

We loaded our belongings onto the carts and left for Azizpur.

We reached our destination by the evening.

We began to settle down in the new village.

We felt strange for a few days but soon got used to the way of life there.

Time is a great healer.

We harvested the crops when they ripened.

We cut grass and fodder in the fields for our cattle and calves.

Babu Ram opened a small shop, where he would sit in his spare time. Besides provisions, he stocked slippers, shoes, etc., in the shop. When his stock was exhausted, he would go to Lahore to replenish it. As this was the only shop in the area, business was brisk.

While living in this village, Babu Ram was blessed with a son who was named Munni Lal.

Everyone in the family was happy about the addition.

We earned quite a lot while living in Azizpur.

The savings that Babu Ram made were sent to our maternal uncle who lived in a nearby village, Karial. Two of our maternal uncles had already gone across to India. The maternal uncle on this side usually remitted funds by money order to his brothers in India, and we left our savings with him so that when we went to India, our uncle would send them to us.

We had been living in Azizpur for more than one and a half years now.

One day, when Babu Ram went to Lahore to make purchases for his shop, he learnt that the Indian government had set up a refugee camp from where the Hindus left in Pakistan were being sent across to India.

Babu Ram met the camp-in-charge.

He related our family's story to him.

The camp-in-charge advised my brother to arrange to reach Lahore railway station where a military van would be available, which would take the family to the camp.

Having found out what he needed to, Babu Ram returned home.

Once again, deliberations began about going to India.

This time, Chacha had made up his mind that our native land was no longer ours. Our country was India. He persuaded others to accompany us.

After some days, we packed our belongings.

We informed the choudhries that we would be leaving for India in a day or two.

A day before leaving the village, Babu Ram went to Lahore and informed the camp-in-charge that we would be arriving in Lahore after two days.

We settled all our accounts with our neighbours. We hired two tongas from the nearby village for fifteen rupees each. They were to take us to Shakargarh railway station.

Chacha had loaned two hundred rupees to a choudhry of the village. He requested him to pay back the money a day before we were to leave. The choudhry agreed to give Chacha the money early in the morning before we left.

That same evening, Punjab Das was sitting with his friends in the village. He overheard some persons whispering to one another that the Hindus were leaving the next morning and that when they crossed the outskirts of the village, they would loot them at a desolate place.

Punjab Das returned home. He shared this information with Chacha and other members of the family, but they paid no heed to it. They thought that the situation had changed for the better. Punjab Das said that he would leave the village at night before the rest of the family and that he should be given some money. If they were really looted on the way, then the money with him would stand them in good stead. The family paid no heed to this also. But still, they gave him twenty or twenty-five rupees. Others in the family also handed him some money—forty to fifty rupees—for safekeeping.

No one knew when Punjab Das woke up and when he left the house. When we got up in the morning, he had already departed.

The tongas arrived early in the morning.

We loaded our belongings.

The two elderly ladies were seated in one tonga. My elder brother's wife was seated in the other tonga because she was pregnant again. Others carried some belongings on their heads. We left for Shakargarh at about 7 a.m.

The village folk gave us a happy send-off. Though their hearts were sad at our leaving, they could understand the pain in our hearts too. It was very difficult to part with those who were our own, but things had come to such a pass that parting was inevitable.

Time changes many colours. Suddenly our own people become strangers.

Our family group once again set out for India. The destination was far away, but our determination was firm this time.

A mud road connected Sialkot with Shakargarh. There was a forest on both sides of the road. Hardly any motor vehicles plied on the road.

Everyone was excited because we knew that this time our immediate destination was close: Shakargarh railway station. Then we would go on to Lahore before finally making it to *our* country.

Everything was moving smoothly.

But, oh, bad luck again. The same thing happened that had happened earlier. Just two miles away from Shakargarh, some rogues suddenly came out of the forest. They held swords and axes. They stopped our tongas and led them to the side of the road. They surrounded us. They looted from us whatever we had. The tongas were also offloaded. They ordered us to pay more money to the tonga-drivers if we wished to continue our journey. And if we did not pay, then we would have to carry our belongings on our heads and walk.

Then the rogues disappeared into the jungle.

We were left crying in desperation.

We had been looted once again.

We had nothing to pay to the tonga-drivers.

We asked them to go back.

Without the tongas, our biggest worry was how to transport the elderly ladies. They were looking at everyone helplessly.

Babu Ram took a sheet and tied its ends to a wooden staff so it hung like a sling and made Grandmother slide into it. Two persons placed either end of the staff on their shoulders so that they could carry Grandmother. The other old lady was lifted by Babu Ram on his back. We downsized our belongings right there, leaving certain articles on the roadside. We then carried on.

We reached the Shakargarh railway station with great difficulty.

We turned hopeful when we found Punjab Das there because he had some money.

Thanks to that money, we bought our tickets.

Chacha hoped that the choudhry who owed him money would come to the railway station to pay it back before the train left. But he did not fulfil his promise.

Two hundred rupees was not a small amount in those days.

After we bought our tickets with the money that Punjab Das had with him, we had nothing left to spend.

Finally, Chacha asked all of us to leave and said that he would return to the village, get the money from the choudhry and leave by train the next day.

The train moved towards Lahore, and Chacha, towards the village.

When we reached Lahore, military vehicles were waiting outside the railway station. Babu Ram met the military officers. As planned, the vehicles took us to the Hindu refugee camp.

A tent was issued to us. Food and water to drink were provided.

Everything seemed to be all right, but we were all worried about Chacha. If the camp officers did not permit Babu Ram to receive Chacha at the station, what would happen? Such thoughts plagued our minds.

The night passed somehow.

In the morning, Babu Ram met the camp-in-charge and related to him what had happened the previous day. Ignoring the rules, the officer permitted him to go to the railway station.

The train was due to arrive at 5 p.m.

Babu Ram reached the station. The train was late.

When it finally arrived, Chacha was nowhere to be seen.

All the passengers came out and left for their homes, but Babu Ram kept looking for Chacha. Worry filled his mind. Maybe Chacha had come out of the train, but he had missed spotting him. Had there been some trouble in the village? Was Chacha robbed by someone on the way? Had he been physically hurt?

It was 10 p.m. but Babu Ram had not found Chacha.

He returned alone to the camp.

All the members of the family were greatly worried, but they could do nothing except wait for him.

Bebe's tears would not stop falling. Both the old ladies were also very worried.

Babu Ram went to the station regularly for two or three days, but Chacha did not come.

The hope of his arrival was receding.

Then, on our fifth day in the camp, we had to leave Pakistan and cross over to India.

At last, our papers were prepared, and we were put on a train.

As the train moved, everyone's eyes were fixed on the buildings, lanes and people of Lahore.

As we looked on, the place of birth of our past generations seemed to be moving away from us. Memories were churning in our minds. Our hearts sank at the thought that we would not be able to see

Lahore again, and it was indeed our bad luck that we never could.

Lahore was being left far behind.

Amritsar was approaching.

Thoughts of Chacha were worrying us.

Finally, we reached Amritsar—that is, our country, Hindustan.

Though Amritsar was not a new place to us—our family had often visited Amritsar—this time, the city appeared to be in a new form. It had a different complexion. Of belongingness. What had been another country had become our own and what was ours had become others'. Strange are the ways of providence! Ordinary humans cannot fathom them.

We were taken to a refugee camp.

It was near the Amritsar railway station.

We stayed there for a few days.

Many other families like us were also there.

Meanwhile, our papers were prepared.

Every day, we looked for Chacha among the passengers coming from Lahore. But our efforts to find him proved futile.

Chacha did not come. There was no news about him.

After four or five days, the camp authorities asked us if we knew where we wanted to move on to. We could either go to the refugee camps set up by the government or carry forward on our own.

Our uncle's family was living in a village called Babbri Bhumbli Dhariwal, which was in the Gurdaspur district. Therefore, as we had decided earlier, we requested the authorities to put us on a train to Dhariwal.

Our request was agreed to.

Soon, we were sitting with the family of our other uncle, Vidhia Ram, in their house.

We embraced one another and shed tears.

We were meeting again after about two years.

Taya had vacated a room for us.

We were very hard up. We had no money at all. We had been looted thrice.

The most pressing problem that stared us demonically in the face in our own country was how to meet the household expenses.

How to fill the bellies of the members of the family?

Two

We were living in the village of Babbri Bhumbli.

Charan and I were still children. We were not able to earn a living.

Babu Ram and Punjab Das began to work for daily wages at Dhariwal. What was earned was spent on the needs of the family.

Famine had befallen that area in those days.

Rotis of gram flour and gram dal were eaten three times a day.

There was no other crop.

Critical conditions prevailed. There was despondence all around. There was no ray of hope anywhere. There was total darkness. Still, the family's hope to see light did not die.

Bebe would send Charan and me to Dhariwal, putting baskets of dried dung-cakes on our heads to sell.

We sold dung-cakes in the lanes of Dhariwal and earned six annas—or even eight annas on some days—and returned home.

We spent one anna each on our mid-day meal. This continued for many days.

During those days, Babu Ram was blessed with a daughter.

Our grandmother also passed away.

Nature plays strange games. Someone is born somewhere; another is dying elsewhere. But this is the law of nature. Life goes on its own way. We have to follow the dictates of life. Life never follows us. It begins on its own and dies on its own. What a wonderful life! Some come out victorious every time; some face defeat at each instance. Gain and loss are integral parts of life.

The other old lady who had been living with us was taken away by her son to his own home. The members of their family were getting properly settled.

All the members of our family, however, were struggling to survive, but the scale leaned heavily towards life.

One day, we received a letter written by Chacha from Pakistan.

Love to everyone.

I am all right here. All of you must be worried. You must have waited for me that day, but allow me to explain what happened to me.

I walked from Shakargarh railway station and reached the village in the evening. I met the choudhry who had borrowed money from me. When I asked him why he had not come to the railway station, he said that he had rushed there, but the train had left before he reached the station. He paid back the money. I went to your maternal uncle's village, Karial, and gave him the money. I related our story to him. He gave me five hundred and fifty rupees that had been left with him. The next day, to cross the border, we left at about 4 or 5 a.m. Your maternal uncle had with him a man from the village. That man had a relative in a village near the border. We had to stay overnight there and cross over the next day. We were about four to six miles away from that village when four or five persons surrounded us in a desolate place. They thrashed us and robbed me of the five hundred rupees that I had. I had hidden two hundred rupees in the hem of the sheet around my waist. We raised a hue and cry. They all took to their heels. Many people gathered there. Some of them knew your maternal uncle. At their insistence, a report was lodged at the police station. I have been to the police station three or four times but there is no information so far about the looters.

I am remitting two hundred rupees by money order. Let me know when it is received. When those people are found and our money is returned, I will join you.

Jai Hind

Love
Keshva Ram

We felt very happy knowing that Chacha was well.

We received a money order for two hundred rupees after a few days.

Those two hundred rupees proved to be our life support. Our family felt a restoration of spirits. We began to bubble with energy.

Babu Ram, Punjab Das and Taya's two sons together set up furnaces for turning wood into coal.

Charan and I worked for a farmer, Zamindar Gulzar Singh, as servants.

We got two quintals of grain every six months, in addition to two meals a day. We were given rotis of wheat and maize. Both of us were very happy as we no longer had to eat gram flour rotis.

Our job was to take the cattle out for grazing, cut grass and fodder, and throw away the rubbish.

Gulzar Singh's family included an elderly person, Sardar Inder Singh, who loved me very much. He taught me Gurmukhi and took great care that I should not be in any discomfort. Still, I was always afraid of the other members of their family. This fear was perhaps due to the lack of a sense of belonging to a particular place or some other cause buried deep inside me. But fear it was, no doubt.

Fear is present in the entire universe. That any person could be free of it forever is not within the realm of possibility. And man is considered to be the most conscious creature. Therefore, he must be more fearful than other beings. Sheikh Farid has broadly described fifty types of fear that man suffers from.

Oftentimes, one not knowing anything about fear remains unaware of it. Those who are very wise fear more than those who are not so wise because they worry about negative possibilities more than ordinary people. They are afraid of consequences and thus hesitate to act.

One morning, I was cutting fodder on the *toka*—a chopping machine—when a booklet containing Saint Dhanna's tale in verse was accidentally chopped with the fodder. This book used to be read with great joy by Inder Singh's younger brother, Kishan Singh. After reading the book, he would keep it in the machine room.

Evening had set in. Kishan Singh was looking for the booklet. I was standing near him. He asked me about the book. I told him nothing because of the fear of what they would do to me should the truth be known. I kept quiet. I was terribly afraid and prayed to God to let the day pass peacefully.

God was kind.

Elder brother Punjab Das came in. He had just returned from Amritsar and had swung by to take me home.

He began to gossip with Kishan Singh. As they were talking, the booklet was forgotten amid other matters quickly occupying the foreground. The fear hovering over my head flew away for the time being.

I heaved a sigh of relief.

I went home with my brother.

On reaching home, I put my head in my mother's lap and cried bitterly, but I did not tell her about the chopping of the booklet. Bebe realized that something was weighing heavily on her son's mind. She asked me again and again what the matter was, and I finally told her. She embraced me tightly. It is only a mother who can read the minds of her children, plainly peering into their pain and worries, without being told.

'Don't worry. The sardar will not say anything. It was only a book.'

My fear dissipated for good upon hearing these words of reassurance from my mother's mouth.

While living in Gulzar Singh's house, I got the opportunity to read many tales, including those of Puran Bhagat, Sassi Punnu, Heer, Roop Basant, Shamo Naar, etc.

When I went home, the members of our family listened to the tales I sang for them. I would borrow one tale or the other from Kishan Singh to take home to read.

At first, I would sleep in Gulzar Singh's house at night. Later, I began to go home after eating my evening meal. I would only stay back on the nights when the sugarcane crusher had to be worked.

The crusher worked till 11 or 12 p.m. The sugarcane juice was boiled, and later, small balls or lumps of jaggery were made from it.

Along with the sardars' sons, some other boys also used to work with us. They kept a watch over the jaggery at night. They also began to distil country liquor at night.

A still was set up either at home or in the fields, wherever space could be found.

During the day, they peeled the sugarcane. At night, they boiled the sugarcane juice for preparing jaggery. They also heated the still to make liquor.

I and two others were asked to insert the canes into the crusher. Once, at midnight, the sardars' sons and their companions began to drink the liquor they had distilled. Two or three others from the village also joined them. When they left, they took three or four bottles of liquor with them. Two bottles or so were hidden under a haystack. I saw them do it.

I fell asleep after some time.

Throughout the night, I kept dreaming about the liquor bottles.

The next day, I thought about how the boys, when drunk, appeared quite changed. Why? Their way of walking and talking would alter.

Henceforth, they would cool the liquor distilled every night and drink it. Then they would sing Heer and Mahiya. They worked very energetically the next day. They became very active.

One of the boys working with me told me that it was all the effect of the liquor. It intoxicated. And they acted the way they did because of the intoxication.

Liquor seemed to be quite wonderful; I kept thinking about it.

I had never drunk liquor, but I wanted to. Why not try it just once? Let me experience how it felt to get drunk.

One day, before taking the cattle out to graze, I thought that the liquor distilled the previous night should be tasted, enjoyed.

I hid the bottle under my towel.

I had my meal.

Before leaving, I requested the sardarni for a little ball of jaggery, two rotis and some pickle.

I was quite excited about trying the liquor.

It was getting difficult to wait.

Finally, I stealthily filled half a glass with liquor, added some water and gulped it all down in one go.

It went in, tearing my insides.

It was so bitter—like poison.

So this is...liquor, I thought as I tasted it.

I had a bite of jaggery and felt a little relieved.

The taste in my mouth changed, but the jaggery added to the intoxication.

As usual, I held a long bamboo staff, untethered the cattle and drove them towards the fields.

The cattle followed the usual path, but I deviated. My steps were unsteady.

After about ten minutes, I was fully drunk. The liquor was hitting my brain. I failed to understand what was happening within me. I felt quite upset.

Then I felt energetic—fully excited.

My feet began to dither. I felt giddy. The earth and the sky seemed to be swirling. It was a strange feeling. It seemed as if I was flying without wings. I galloped and jumped on to the back of a grey buffalo.

When I looked ahead, I could see the backs of all the cattle. There were horns everywhere. It was a horrifying spectacle. It seemed as if I had reached the Yamaloka.

Holding the staff as I sat on the buffalo's back, I considered myself no less than Yamaraja. My mind was suffused with excitement.

I placed one end of the staff on the ground near the foreleg of the buffalo. As the buffalo walked and his hind leg drew level with the staff, I again placed it near the foreleg. I enjoyed doing so again and again.

I don't know what happened next, but suddenly, as I placed the staff near the foreleg of the buffalo, the upper end caught me in my belly. As the buffalo moved ahead, I was lifted above its back. The buffalo moved further ahead, and I fell down with a thud.

I stood up and moved my hand over my belly and found that everything was all right, but I was in severe pain.

Still, I felt that my royal ride was not yet complete.

I tried to jump on to the back of the buffalo. Despite several attempts, if I tried to mount from one side, I fell down on the other. Ultimately, I succeeded in riding the buffalo.

By now, I was more in control of myself. I enjoyed the royal ride. What a joy it was!

The buffalo marched on until it stopped at its usual place to graze.

I dismounted and sat down with the other herdsmen.

There were five or seven of them. Two of them were older than me. These were the two who would beat me in wrestling.

The intoxication had reached its peak. I was about to lose my head. I felt like doing something. I had drunk liquor. I was drunk. I should tell the others. I should show it off! I stood up and challenged the two herdsmen to wrestle.

'If anyone has drunk his mother's milk, he should come wrestle with me.'

Fully drunk, I was in a mood to tickle them.

The boys kept quiet in response. They were looking at me strangely. They couldn't understand how this deer had turned into a lion.

At last, I told them that I was drunk. They had no need to fear me. Then we began to wrestle together.

The economic condition of the family was gradually improving.

I no longer had to work at Gulzar Singh's place.

I had begun to work for my own family.

Around the same time, Babu Ram's eldest son, Munni Lal, suddenly fell seriously ill.

Unrest erupted in the house.

Babu Ram had to leave his work mid-day and return home.

The boy was taken for treatment to many places. But the medicines had no effect.

And then, he passed away one day.

Mourning gripped the house. But what could be done? The inevitable had happened.

During the treatment of his son, Babu Ram's business of turning wood into coal had slackened. He continued to suffer losses until the business finally shut down.

Meanwhile, Chacha had joined us from Pakistan.

The time to harvest the wheat crop was approaching.

Chacha, Babu Ram and Punjab Das worked very hard to reap the crop.

The women of the family gathered the cut wheat ears and brought them home.

In a few days' time, we were able to collect a good quantity of grain.

Things improved for the family once again.

Charan and I also got two quintals of grain each from Gulzar Singh, for whom we had worked last year.

The famine in the area ceased with the end of the famine, so to say, in our house.

Besides the gram pulse and roti, many other and new delicacies began to be prepared.

Charan had grown up.

He began to share in the work of the family.

He was later engaged by another family to work for them.

The work on the railway line between Mukerian and Pathankot had begun in those days.

Punjab Das started working there.

After working for five to six months, he came home with four or five hundred rupees.

That money was spent on Punjab Das' marriage.

After that, Babu Ram also went to work in the railways.

Some time later, quarrels erupted among the refugees from Pakistan living in Babbri village.

The main cause of trouble was the population census conducted by the government.

The Punjab government wanted the people to declare Punjabi to be their mother tongue; while the Hindu refugees insisted that Hindi was their mother tongue, the Sikh refugees stated the same of Punjabi.

This gave rise to quarrels and infighting.

Both sides went to the police and courted arrest.

After some days, they made peace, but the landowners, still upset, forbade the refugees from using their fields to cut grass and fodder or answer nature's call.

Troubled by such restrictions, many refugees began to move to the cities.

To them, living in the cities appeared to be safer than living in the villages.

One day, Chacha went to see Babu Ram and Punjab Das. In those days, they were working in Chakk Bharaiyaan village, which was on the

Mukerian—Pathankot line. He met the people of the neighbouring villages there.

A close friend of Chacha, Bachitar Ram, lived in a nearby village, Chakk Naraini. He invited him to his house. Chacha liked the people of this area very much.

'Dear friend, get some land for our family in a nearby village so that I can bring them here from Babbri. The rift between the landlords and the refugees is continuing there,' Chacha said to Bachitar.

The next day, Bachitar Ram took Chacha to meet the Rajput choudhries of Chakk Bharaiyaan.

By chance, the choudhries were also refugees and came from the villages quite near ours. Chacha quickly developed a rapport with them.

They choudhries gave Chacha a house that had been vacated by a Muslim family.

Chacha thanked the choudhries profusely.

He returned to Babbri.

Soon after, our family began to make preparations to leave.

A few days later, we all moved to Chakk Bharaiyaan.

This village became our home forever.

Both Babu Ram and Punjab Das continued to work in the railways.

Chacha looked after the cattle. He brought grass and fodder for them.

But by this time, his health had begun to suffer. He coughed all the time. He started undergoing treatment.

Bebe worried a lot about Chacha.

Charan and I had grown up by then.

Our family sent us to graze the cattle.

In those days, we reared goats as well.

We worked sometimes with a mason for daily wages.

Things were improving for the family.

Punjab Das had been promoted from a labourer to a supervisor. His salary had increased.

Taya's sons living in Babbri had also begun to work in the railways.

The train service from Jalandhar to Pathankot started in due course.

The country was making progress. The prosperity of our family was also increasing. The members of the family had ruddy cheeks now. Their faces bloomed. Everyone had enough food to fill their bellies to their satisfaction.

After some time, Babu Ram left the railways, but Punjab Das got a regular job in the sector on the Joginder Nagar line.

Charan also worked with Punjab Das in the railways for about six months.

I was not yet old enough to get into service.

I was still sent out to graze cattle and goats.

When I returned in the evenings, I would bring back a bundle of fuel wood, which was used in the kitchen.

The boys of other farmers also went with me to graze goats.

They were older than me—and more mischievous also. Every day, they committed some mischief or the other.

Sometimes, they plucked mangoes and stole melons or corn cobs or sesame or some other thing.

One day, a Jat boy from a neighbouring village joined us in the jungle with his goats.

By chance, a goat, separated from someone's flock, got into our flock. Mischief began to brew in the boys' minds. They made me join in their plans.

Four of us slaughtered the goat and divided the meat among us.

In the evening, we returned to our respective homes, each with our share of the meat.

When my family asked me where the meat had come from, I put the blame on the three other boys.

This meat was cooked in our house for various meals over the next four to five days.

A few days later, one of our goats fell ill and died soon after. The family mourned.

I was blamed for its death because I had stolen someone else's goat.

They believed that had I not done the evil act, our goat would not have died.

'God has punished us for the sin. We never asked you to slaughter someone else's goat and get meat for us. An innocent animal was killed.'

On that day, I swore that I would never steal or bring home stolen property.

It was the month of October. The sesame crop had ripened in the fields. The farmers had cut the sesame and spread it in the fields to dry.

A boy from our village and I had gone near their fields to graze our goats.

Mischief simmered in our minds. Both of us began to thresh the sesame. We were still doing this when the owner turned up. He caught hold of me. He slapped me four or five times and then gave me a few blows as well. The other boy fled as he saw me being beaten.

For the crime of stealing, the farmer put me to work in the field to thresh maize. The first sheaf was thrown before me by the farmer, and after that, I myself continued to remove the sheaves from the stack and thresh them. The stack was thirty to forty feet away.

I did not have the courage to run away.

That village was four or five miles away from our village.

In the evening, I went to the farmer's house carrying a big basket full of cobs.

He advised me not to commit theft again and let me off.

I took to my heels and got home.

My family did not know about my prank. My friend had not told them.

I felt greatly relieved.

Both of us were very annoyed with the farmer for catching us red-handed and then thrashing me and making me thresh his maize. To avenge this, we planned to repeat our misconduct. We settled with a shopkeeper near the railway station to sell the sesame to him. We told him that we would come to the shop rather late, so he should keep it open. The shopkeeper readily agreed because he was keen to buy the sesame at the 'theft rate' and then sell it at a big profit.

Money is such a thing that at the sight of it, everyone, rich or poor, gets tempted.

That night, we threshed five to six kilos of sesame.

We knew that the shopkeeper would under-weigh it and then pay us a lower rate. So we added about two kilos of sand to the sesame.

When we reached the shop, we found the shopkeeper waiting for us impatiently.

He gave us seven rupees for the entire lot.

We took two rupees on the spot and told him to hold on to five rupees for us so that we could take it from him later to spend during the Dussehra fair.

At last, the festival arrived.

Both of us went to the shopkeeper, but his intentions had turned bad. He said that I had taken the remaining five rupees from him the next day.

I tried my best to convince my friend that I was innocent, but he was annoyed with me and began to regard me as a dishonest person. A crack developed in our friendship. It took a lot of time to mend it.

Many such things happen in life that are beyond one's control. Sometimes, you have to undergo punishment for something not done by you.

In those days, a lot of importance was attached to festivals, especially the Lohri festival. Many delicacies were prepared in the house that day.

When a son was born in the family or a son was married or some progressive people were blessed with a daughter or a daughter's marriage had taken place, the family celebrated Lohri. They would distribute sweets and savouries among their friends and relatives. These included *bhatura*, dried corn, peanuts, *rioris* (balls of sugar paste covered with sesame seed), *chirwarai* (soaked, beaten and salted rice), *batasha* (sugar drops), etc.

In the evening, we would get together, collect firewood and make a bonfire to propitiate Lohri.

A week before Lohri, a group of us would start going from door to door in the village to "collect lohri" for our piggy banks.

In those days, the villages experienced severe cold. From mid-December to mid-January, the days were short and evenings set in very early. Early in the morning, the fodder would be covered with frost. As we cut grass and fodder for the cattle, our hands would turn blue with cold, but we never complained. We knew that if we dallied, we would not be permitted to go out in the evening to collect lohri.

Sometimes, we went to the neighbouring villages as well. Occassionally, we even had a drummer with us. Holding bags open in our hands to collect flour and rice, we'd start seeking lohri with a particular rhyme:

Sunder mundriai … ho
Tera kaun vichara… ho
Dulla Bhatti wala … ho
Dulley di dhee vyahee ... ho
Nau man shakkar payee … ho
Kudi da lal dupatta … ho
Kudi da nanna natha … ho

O beautiful dame!
Who cares for you

Dulla Bhatti
Dulla's daughter was wed
Given nine maunds of sugar
The girl had a red scarf
The girl's grandfather fled

On the other hand, the village girls would seek lohri with a different song:

Kaud kabaddiya kaudi deh
Kaudi deh
Virai de ghar vahuti deh
Vahuti deh
Virai di vahuti sohni
Sohni
Uhdai mathe dauni
Dauni
Virai di vahuti sohni
Sohni

Give us cowries O kabaddi player
Give us cowries
Give a bride to the brother
Give a bride
Brother's bride is pretty
A pendant on her forehead
Brother's bride is pretty

Sometimes, a boy from our group would playact as a deer, for which we'd paint him red and yellow and tie sticks to his head. A rope was then tied around his neck and arms, both ends of which were held by another boy. The boy-turned-deer would hold two sticks in his hands and run back and forth on entering a house, the tiny bells on his anklets jingling. He would hit the door with his sticks and the others would sing:

Shaava hiran shaava
Bhan sut paahva
Hiran maari takkar
De maai shakkar

Wonderful deer
Would break a leg
The deer collided
Give us sugar, mother

Most people gave us flour or rice. Some gave five or ten paisa also. Very rarely was anyone so generous as to give us half a rupee or a rupee. Some houses gave us even peanuts and sugar drops.

Some lads who were old enough to grow moustaches would get a peg or two to drink.

The drummer would beat the drum and the boys would dance merrily in the courtyards of the houses.

If, however, a family refused to give us any offering altogether, they'd be subjected to an acerbic rhyme designed particularly for the occasion:

Hukke utte hukka
Eh ghar bukha

One hookah atop another
This house is empty

If there had been a death in a house, the family did not partake in the celebrations, nor did anyone go to them to collect lohri.

After all the flour and rice were collected and sold, the proceeds were added to the coins already received. Everyone would get their share of two or three rupees.

Those were wonderful childhood days. We would lead our cattle to the hollows and dunes of the village. The cattle were left to roam while we relaxed under the cool shade of a mango or banyan tree. Sometimes, we turned the large branches of the trees into cots. We plucked mangoes by hurling stones and pebbles at them. Sometimes, we carried with us hooks to fish in the pond. We jumped into the pond and bathed. We plucked sweet berries from bushes in deserted places. We also got sugarcane, melons, watermelons and *kakari*, a variety of cucumber, from the fields.

As the sun gradually went down the horizon, we would prepare to return our destination. We quickly gathered the cattle as we wanted to get home at the earliest. We felt a great peace upon reaching our destination. If we were delayed, Bebe would come and wait for us on the outskirts of the village. Finding her waiting for us, we would run up to her and hug her. It was a wonderful, peaceful feeling.

As the cattle walked, they swished their tails, whisking away flies. The tinkling of the little bells around their necks sounded sweetly melodious. The animals would tease one another. They rubbed against one another as they moved. They ran races, jumped and danced. They bellowed loudly as they moved towards the house. It seemed as if they were speaking of the day gone by. We would string together any fish we had caught and carry it with us. Keeping bundles of grass and fodder balanced on our heads, we followed the cattle.

If we had been thrashed by a farmer because the cattle had laid waste to his field, or we had been caught stealing mangoes or melons, then we would walk home silently, but if we were in a good mood, or if the weather was pleasant, we would sing songs. Sometimes, we would ride on the back of a buffalo.

Outside the village was a large mango tree, which spread wide like a huge umbrella, and several banyan trees, their roots dangling from the branches like sparse beards. Birds and other creatures had made their nests in these trees. These trees were like villages for them. Crows, parrots, kites, bats, doves, sparrows, koels and nightingales had made their homes in them. In the trunks of these trees were holes in which lived lizards, rats, mongoose and snakes.

As the evening set in, the birds chirped their way back to their nests. Their hopping and chirping made a wonderful spectacle. The crickets and grasshoppers hiding in the hollows of the bushes and trees made shrill noises, as if sounding the bugle of the evening setting in. The *aarti* in the temple on the bank of the rain drain and the singing of Gurbani in the village gurdwara could be heard. The fragrance of incense spread all around. The sweetness of the Gurbani entered our ears. All this combined to create a wonderful evening.

As we approached the village, we were greeted by twinkling lamps illuminating the many houses in our view. Milky-white smoke rising from the hearths flew skywards. Children played in the lanes, laughing, crying, dancing, jumping and merrymaking—full of life and enjoying their carefree childhood. The elders played cards or gossiped outside the Dehri Mata temple or played with their grandchildren, enjoying the afternoon of their lives.

I had begun to grow a moustache. I would sometimes go with my friends to the nearby town of Pathankot to watch a movie. I would also go to the Baisakhi and Dussehra fairs.

One day, a boy from the neighbouring village enrolled in the army.

I too began to dream day and night of joining the army.

I would find out where and when recruitment for the army was taking place.

Three

Whenever I heard about an army recruitment camp being held somewhere, I would go there. Sometimes, my chest was not wide enough. Sometimes, my breathing was laboured. Sometimes, I lagged behind in the long jump. And so, I was not recruited.

Indeed, I was upset. I felt that I would never be recruited. But I did not lose heart.

Then came the day when my dream was fulfilled.

It happened like this. A recruitment camp was being held in a nearby town. I too rushed there and joined the queue of hopeful lads.

Those whose weight and height met the requirements were made to sit on one side. I was one of them. That day, twenty boys were to be enrolled.

We were asked to frog-jump. Then, we had to stand on one leg.

Many of the boys could jump but could not stand on one leg.

One or two of them did manage and were taken aside.

Suddenly, I observed that a boy was stealthily standing on both legs, but he shouted out that he had been standing on one leg. He too was selected.

'Sir, I did it! I did it!' I too shouted out.

On hearing me, the officer made me stand in the row of those to be enrolled.

After some time, the officer completed the necessary paperwork.

I was enrolled in the army.

It was the beginning of a new life.

A new dawn.

A new aspiration.

I returned home.

My family was overjoyed to hear about my recruitment.

Chacha and Bebe were the happiest of all because their little gem was going to make a success of his life.

The next day, accompanied by three boys from the neighbouring villages who had also been recruited, I set out for the headquarters of the Bengal Engineers in Roorkee.

We reached there in the evening and had our attendance marked.

Another boy and I were sent to the company platoon.

Our training started the next day.

The training was very difficult. There were about seventy boys in the platoon. We were made to run the whole day. Sometimes, we were made to run races at night also. If a single recruit erred, the whole platoon was punished. We were made to hold rifles and raise our arms above our heads. We had to take five rounds or so of the training ground. Each round was one and a half miles. We panted for breath. We were often on the verge of crying. This continued for about six months.

Gradually, I became quite fit, and my body developed very well. I had good stamina.

We began to be assigned duties. Sometimes, it was day duty, and sometimes, night duty. We missed home very much; occasionally, we couldn't help crying.

Happiness and unhappiness presented themselves to us side by side.

It is a very strange feeling when happiness and unhappiness intermingle.

One day, I was crying but on seeing an officer heading towards me, I quickly wiped away my tears. The officer came up to me and said, 'Young man, this crying will last for some days only. Early on, I too had cried like this, but everything turned out well. Don't take all this to heart.'

After that day, I never cried.

Eventually, I passed the recruitment tests and became a true and regular soldier.

I was still in Roorkee when I received a letter informing me about the marriage of my elder brother Charan Das.

I went home on six days' leave.

After the wedding, I returned to Roorkee.

I received a telegram in March 1958 informing me of the sad demise of Chacha. I was very sad, but who can fight against nature? And if one does try to fight, who has ever won? I thought it better to bow before nature.

I tried my best, but I could not get leave.

I could not be present at the time of Chacha's last rites.

When Charan Das and his wife Shanti went to Haridwar to immerse his ashes, I joined them.

The following day, I returned to Roorkee, and Charan Das and his wife returned to the village.

On 4 April 1958, I, along with three other soldiers, was sent to the training centre in Secunderabad.

We trained there for six months.

While there, I went to Hyderabad also.

When we felt homesick, we would all get together, and my fellow soldiers often insisted that I sing something for them.

I would feel lighter when I sang, especially a particular song that warmed all our hearts.

Some days ago, on a dark night
I was on quarter guard duty

Duty hours were ten to twelve
It was pitch dark all around
It was a freezing dark night
Only my rifle gave me company
The memory of someone held me
Like a well-bathed picture of love
The fragrance of her body spread around
In my imagination I approached her
What brings you here O my mate?
She said as I stood near her
I have come to meet you, my dear
I smiled looking at her blooming face
As I put the garland in my hands
Around her beautiful neck
The duty officer stood behind me
He had seen everything
I had simply lost my wits, friends
I could think of only this, friends
It is my mistake, sir, I am sorry.

On 5 October 1958, I boarded the train to return to Roorkee.

It was a Sunday.

We reached Nagpur on Monday evening. The train halted there for some time.

We ate our meal at the station before returning to our compartment.

The train had not yet moved when a fellow soldier quietly said to me that he needed a cigarette. He asked me to buy him a packet.

I briefly got off and went to a stall on the platform. Meanwhile, the train began to move. I ran after it, but, instead of my own compartment, I jumped into the last compartment of the train.

There was no vacant seat there.

To while away the time till the train reached the next station, I went to stand at the door to watch the scenery go by.

I don't know how it happened, but, as the train was running at high speed, I slipped and fell.

I regained consciousness the next day.

I saw a doctor and asked him where I was. I was told that I was in the Ambala Military Hospital.

I didn't remember what had happened; whether I had fallen off the train or I had been injured in the train itself. My treatment went on for five days.

Then a fellow soldier told me that some other passengers had seen me falling off the train.

They had raised a hue and cry.

Someone had pulled the chain for the emergency brake.

The train had stopped at some distance from where I had fallen.

On enquiry, the guard had been told that an army man had fallen from the train.

Some passengers had then disembarked from the train and run back to look for me.

They had found me about half a kilometre away.

I had been lying on the railway tracks. Given that I had fallen off the last compartment, the wheels had not passed over me.

My fellow soldiers had also reached the spot with the other passengers. They had recognized me. The guard had then reversed the train's course. Still unconscious, I had been put on the same train. The guard had kept me in his own cabin.

The train had moved again.

The guard had judged that my condition had been critical.

At the next station, he had sent word to the Ambala Military Hospital that a soldier had been injured. The train had reached Ambala at 10 p.m.

The hospital had sent an ambulance to the railway station. Meanwhile, my fellow soldiers had put some money in my pocket. A spare blanket had been kept with me.

As soon as the train had halted, I had been taken to the ambulance and driven to the hospital.

There they had discovered that I had had a simple head injury. Treatment had then begun.

After recovering, I left for Roorkee. My fellow soldiers had already informed the training centre about my accident.

The day after I arrived, I appeared before the commanding officer.

I told him the whole story.

The commander embraced me.

My fellow soldiers also celebrated my return.

I wrote to my family, telling them everything.

They got upset. The wrote back and asked me to visit home, but I could not get leave despite requesting it several times.

Soon after, I was transferred to Allahabad.

After some days, I was sanctioned a month's leave.

I went home.

My family heaved a sigh of relief on seeing me.

Bebe was extremely happy that her son was safe and sound.

I returned to Allahabad after a month.

I remained in Allahabad from 10 October 1958 to 5 February 1960.

I went home twice on two months' leave each time while I was in Allahabad.

I also participated in the Kumbh Mela there.

People came to the mela from all over the world. I saw the sadhus clad in different ways. The mela was spread over an area of twelve miles. I had a dip at the Triveni Sangam, the confluence of the Ganga, Jamuna and Saraswati rivers.

The mela ended in January.

I was transferred back to Roorkee.

The army had raised a new company there.

I made friends with another soldier, Bhaag Singh. That friendship lasted my entire life. Bhaag Singh belonged to a village near Talwara in District Hoshiarpur.

The new company moved from Roorkee to Ambala.

Bhaag Singh was with me.

Soon, we began to receive letters from our parents about our respective marriages.

My marriage was fixed for 7 February 1961 and Bhaag Singh's for 5 February 1961.

Marriage preparations began. Clothes and other necessities were purchased. We had some memorable photographs taken.

Suddenly, on 5 January 1961, our company was sent to Beas, a town in Amritsar, for a training course on building a bridge.

We had to endure the cold water of the Beas river in the month of January!

The training continued day and night. We shivered all the time. On occasion, it even rained. Only God saved us then. The training lasted a month.

One day, a *vadda khaana,* a great feast served to both officers and soldiers in the Indian Army, was held. Someone told one of the officers that I sang well. The next moment, I was singing a favourite as per his request.

The ties broken,
Driven to sadness
O pretty one, pretty one
What did I gain
By falling in love?
It has rained heavily
The cold has increased
Sitting on the bank
Of the River Beas
O pretty one, pretty one
What did I gain
By falling in love?
Oh! Pretty one, pretty one
What avail, falling in love?

Such get-togethers were held quite frequently. And I was often asked to sing.

The training ended at last, and the company returned to Ambala.

Bhaag Singh and I applied for leave.

Our leave was sanctioned after some days.

Both of us reached home on 27 January 1961.

Soon, the wedding festivities began at my place. Delicacies were being prepared. A shopping spree too was taking place.

There was hustle and bustle in the house.

Preparations for my marriage were in full swing.

On 5 February 1961, my younger sister Bhano Devi's marriage was solemnized.

On 7 February, my marriage party left by train for the nearby town of Purana Bhangala.

I was married to a very pretty and tall girl, Bobby.

When she came to our home, she was renamed Bachno.

My bride was beautiful. Tall and slender. And very good-natured. It seemed my new life with her would be very nice.

I too was perhaps liked by her.

Alas, my leave was cut short abruptly and I was ordered to report back for duty immediately. The company had to proceed to Goa.

I left Bachno at her parents' place.

I proceeded half-heartedly to the Ambala cantonment.

Upon reaching there, I learnt that our company had already left for Goa. After two days, ten soldiers, including me, were also sent to the coastal state. It took us two or three days to finally join our company.

The Goa Operation had begun.

We performed our duty. Our company remained in Goa for about three months.

When we got permission, Bhaag Singh and I went to the bazaar.

We drank country liquor made of cashew nuts. We travelled all over Goa. Wild banana grew in abundance. Cashew was also grown extensively. In 1961, cashew was sold there at one and a half rupees per kilo. Cashew liquor was sold at one rupee a small glass. We drank this liquor to our heart's content. Drinking was prohibited by the company, but like other soldier brothers, I too slipped out to drink.

We saw a television for the first time in Goa. It was at the residence of one of our officers.

Our company returned to Ambala on 1 April 1961.

We roamed around Ambala leisurely. There was hardly a lane or street that we did not visit.

On 5 November 1961, our company was ordered to proceed to Siliguri for the China Operation. We went by train. From there, our convoy reached Binaguri.

Our company was asked to construct roads. Barracks for the soldiers also had to be built. The company's duty was not at the first level to fight at the front but at the third level to build roads and barracks for the soldiers.

Fighting continued for fifteen to twenty days.

Our company remained occupied in building barracks.

In those days, I used to drive a three-tonner. Some other soldiers and I had got a driving licence from Jalpaiguri.

I had thought that after retirement, I would return to my village and buy a vehicle, but the dreams that we have are not necessarily fulfilled. The same happened with me too.

After some days, our company moved to Chalsa near Binaguri. I completed the Lance Naik course there and was promoted from soldier to lance naik. I was made a section commander. Many a time, I was assigned the duty of langar commander as well.

My job was to assign duties to the jawans. I also had to keep a record of who was doing which duty, who had gone on leave, and how many jawans were present in the company. All this data had to be submitted to the company commander by 9 p.m. every night.

Our company moved on to Sikkim in December 1963. We camped in Gangtok, the capital of Sikkim, for a fortnight. From there, we proceeded to the China border.

Our company was camped at a terrible place. The site was on a large rock. We felt very afraid at night. We often got lost in the darkness and could not find our way back to the camp. We had been ordered to ensure that all our movements were noiseless. Everything had to be done silently. Dinner was given to us at 11 p.m. on the first day. Thereafter, we had our meals at 9 p.m. Four soldiers were assigned to each bunker to sleep in at night. The bunkers were well-like pits at the bottom of which was provided space to sleep. Our company had to build roads in the area. The infantry fought at the border. The Corps of Electronics and Mechanical Engineers (EME) ensured that all the weapons and equipment were in proper working condition.

My job was to repair vehicles.

The Army Medical Corps (AMC) was responsible for the treatment of injured jawans.

I was not sanctioned annual leave in 1962.

The following year, due to the ongoing national emergency (1962-1968), I was denied leave once more.

At last, in January 1964, I was granted sixty-six days' leave.

On 6 January, I was sent from Sikkim to the Siliguri military camp.

I prepared the papers for my leave there. My request was granted the next day.

From Siliguri, I passed through Mokamah Ghat, Patna Sahib, Varanasi and Lucknow before ultimately reaching my village.

I was overjoyed to be home.

Henceforth, I remained occupied with household chores. I visited my relatives along with my wife. Being a soldier, my relatives held me in high esteem. Everyone saluted me. Sometimes, I went for a movie with my wife. We attended some weddings too. Sometimes, we just went on an outing. We also arranged many matrimonial alliances.

We were enjoying life thoroughly.

Around that time, another soldier had also returned to the village on leave. He had brought with him some explosives that were hidden in his bed roll. He worked in the GREF (General Reserve Engineer Force), which was responsible for road-building. They blasted hillsides, rocks, etc., with explosives and small grenades.

While he was in the village, the soldier would catch fish with the help of those grenades. He would throw a grenade into a pond or storm drain. The explosion would kill the fish. In the evening, he would fry the fish. Being my neighbour, he would send some fish across to our house as well.

I always tried to stop him from committing this sin.

But he would laugh my admonitions away.

I assisted him in many domestic chores. He too returned the favor. He helped us thatch our roof, and I helped him thatch theirs.

One day, as he was busy thatching his roof, he gave me a grenade to keep at our place for some days. I hid it in the house. I feared lest a child should touch it.

One day, I received a letter from Bhaag Singh that he was coming to visit me.

I still had fifteen or twenty days' leave remaining.

For long, I waited for Bhaag Singh, but he did not come. Finally, it was the last day of my leave. I had to report back to the company on 16 March.

I decided to leave my house on 13 March.

On the night of 12 March, I packed up my bed roll and kept my luggage ready.

Soon, it was the next morning.

I had a bath and got dressed before sitting down for breakfast.

I ate my breakfast.

As I was finishing my meal, I suddenly remembered the grenade I had hidden in the house. I decided to dispose of it lest something untoward should happen later.

I put a towel over my shoulder, held the grenade in my hand and set out for the outskirts of the village.

I spotted an anthill on the way. I thought of dropping the grenade in it. Then I saw a spade and a pick lying nearby. It appeared that the owner of the field in which the anthill was located was planning to clear the anthill from his field. I thought that if I put the grenade in it, the poor man would suffer harm if he used his spade or pick to dig up the anthill.

I changed my mind and moved on.

I reached the same drain where my neighbour killed fish by hurling grenades into the water. I looked at my watch. It was 9 a.m. The train was to leave at 3 p.m.

Evil entered my mind.

I thought of drawing the pin of the grenade and throwing it in the drain. I would kill some fish—enough for a good lunch!

I also realized that I had never done such a thing in the past. Why should I do it now? I used to tell my neighbour, the solider, not to do such a sinful thing. But sin was creeping into my thoughts that day. I tried to change my mind, but the scale leaned towards using the grenade.

The mind is such a thing that it can often defeat us. It is said with good reason that victory over one's mind is the most difficult thing to achieve. So I, too, was defeated by the mischievous mind.

I decided to use the grenade and hurl it into the drain.

I had learned how to use the weapon. The safety fuse in the grenade was six inches long. It had to be pulled out and lit. After it was ignited, there was a brief time lag before the grenade exploded. It was during this brief interval that it had to be hurled away.

I took a matchbox out of my pocket.

I lit a matchstick.

I held the grenade in my left hand.

I tried to light the safety fuse with the matchstick.

I could not see the end of the fuse being ignited.

Suddenly, some smoke rose from the fuse. Before I could hurl it away, a loud explosion took place.

Everything came to a standstill for some moments.

There was a horrible silence.

It was as if time had stopped.

The grenade had exploded in my left hand.

My hand was blown off.

All this happened in a moment or two.

I did not know what had happened.

'I am dying, Bebe…'

Stars appeared before my eyes. Smoke engulfed me. The birds chirping on the tree branches flew away.

My shredded hand dangled at the end of my arm. Blood was flowing profusely. My shirt sleeve and trousers were soaked scarlet. It was a horrible sight.

Some shrapnel had hit the rest of my body also, but those were minor injuries. I had not fallen unconscious.

The explosion was heard far away by those working in the fields. No one could guess what had happened.

Many knew that soldiers did cause such explosions. They went back to work.

I wrapped my injured arm in the towel and reached home.

There was a hue and cry when the family saw I had been seriously injured.

Bachno and Bebe shrieked in horror.

The entire family gathered around me.

No one could guess what had happened.

Many questions danced across their faces.

I wore my uniform trousers with one hand. Then I walked towards the railway station.

Bebe and my brother Babu Ram followed me.

A retired soldier in the village also accompanied me.

We boarded the 11 a.m. train and reached the military hospital in Pathankot.

As soon as I was admitted, I fainted.

This happened because of excessive bleeding.

Four

I regained consciousness at 5 a.m. I was surprised to see patients all around me. I saw some nurses as well. But I did not see anyone from my family. I could not understand what was happening. I had forgotten what had passed the previous day. I did not remember the serious accident I had suffered. Perhaps this was the effect of the medicines.

My eyes shut on their own.

Some members of my family, including my wife and Babu Ram, came to see me at about 10 a.m. Their eyes were full of tears as they asked how I was feeling.

My wife was in a bad state. Her eyes were swollen and cheeks hollow. Many a question clouded her forlorn expression.

She wanted to share her thoughts with me. She wanted to hear from me what had happened and how

I was feeling, but she was crying so much that she was not able to say anything.

Tears were flowing from my eyes, too, like ceaseless streams.

A short while later, a nurse asked my family members to wait outside as it was time for the doctors' visit.

The doctors came and examined me. They gave me a shot and then left. I went to sleep again.

Visitors were allowed to see patients from 12 p.m. to 2 p.m. A stream of visitors came to see me. Relatives kept dropping in. Everyone asked the same question: 'What will happen now?'

Some asked why I had not acted more wisely. Why had I gone to the drain? I used to advise others against committing the sin of blasting fish, and then I had committed the same sin myself.

'Puran, you are such a wise person, who always advised others to do what was right. Where did all your wisdom go? We had pinned so many hopes on you, but you have dashed them all. What will happen now? O God, why have you done this to us?' my elder brother Babu Ram lamented loudly.

I too began to cry bitterly, as did all the others who came to see me.

I listened to everyone and felt ashamed. I could not look anyone in the eye. Visiting hours came to a painful end. Everyone left one by one.

I felt some relief. Their excessive affection for me weighed heavily on my mind, which was consequently in turmoil. All of them were more worried than me about my future. Perhaps this is what is called the relationship of affection.

I lay alone once again in my bed. I glanced at my injured arm. The arm, sans my hand, was wrapped in blood-stained white bandages. The sight made me cry. My left hand had been destroyed. The doctors had stitched up the wounds. It felt very strange to look at my arm.

There was now nothing where there had once been my hand. I felt incomplete—*apuran*. The universe had rendered my name a cruel joke.

I was now a one-handed person—a *tunda*, the maimed one, as people would call me contemptuously.

Crippled.

Incomplete.

I kept crying as I looked at my wounded arm.

What else could I do except cry?

How much water could the eyes hold? It all dried up. It had to dry up ultimately. There was no other way but to bow before His will. But how can the heart be content?

The same question arose in my mind again and again—what would happen to me?

To my life?

To my wife?

My family?
My service?
Many other questions also loomed like ghosts.
Then I dozed off.
Time never forgets its march.
One may die or live, but time goes on unconcerned.
My treatment had begun.

Every day, my family members would come from the village to see me. They sat with me before returning home by the 2 p.m. train.

This continued for many days.

I knew that their round trips would be costing them five to six rupees every day. My income had ceased, while our expenditure had increased. The question of how we would make ends meet was forever on my mind, upsetting me.

So, one day, I told my family that instead of visiting every day, they should come on alternate days to reduce expenses. They agreed—after all, they were busy with their own families—but Bachno insisted on showing up daily. What would she do at home, alone with her worries?

After a few days, it was decided that the others should come only once a week.

Bachno came every day by noon, bringing with her the one-and-a-half-year-old son of my elder brother.

The reason for this was that if there was a child with her, no one would trouble them on the way.

Each day, she would spend an hour and a half with me and return by the 4 p.m. train.

I would go to the railway station to see her off.

Every moment, I tried to read her face.

What was going on in her mind?

What was she feeling?

These thoughts plagued me.

I had heard somewhere that in adverse circumstances, young and beautiful women often left their husbands. I was worried that my wife would leave me. This fear ate me up every day.

Before she leaves me, I should tell her to go back to her parents, I began to think.

How circumstances can turn one's mind in hitherto unthinkable directions.

Of course, all of us are human beings. As circumstances change, our views and behaviour also change. Many knots are untangled, and many are created. Friends grow apart, and strangers come close.

I tried my best to share all this with her, but no words escaped my lips. Such words are so weighty that it is difficult for the tongue to bear them. This is why, perhaps, it is said that words can cause deeper wounds than bullets from a gun. Such wounds can fester throughout one's life, causing unbearable pain. And often, there is no remedy.

There was a small culvert on the way to the railway station. We would sit there almost every day while waiting for the train and share our thoughts. Whatever was churning within me had turned into lava, ready to erupt. When my forbearance had crossed its limits, the lava erupted one day. It had to. How long could I suppress it?

'Look here, listen to me patiently...You may not like what I am going to say. It may shock you. But if I do not say this today, I will breathe my last under its weight. I will be burnt alive in the endless streams of its lava. You should go back to your parents...When two years ago your parents saw me and got you married to me, I was a complete man. I had all my limbs, but now, I am maimed. I may soon be jobless too...You are still young, and very beautiful, and we have had no child so far. I may not be able to take proper care of you. I won't be able to see to all your comforts. People will taunt you, call you a cripple's wife...So if you wish, you can leave me... I will divorce you. Let your parents look for another boy and marry you off again. I can make do even by resorting to begging... If possible, can you forgive me? I will not be able to stand by you...Leave me to my fate...'

It took a lot to spew out everything I was feeling in front of her.

And I had succeeded in doing something very difficult.

I had presented myself as a stone-hearted person. But the reality was starkly different.

The explosion had engulfed everything in sight.

But its heat was felt only by Bachno.

Stunned, she looked at me.

Her complexion turned pale.

She remained stupefied for some time.

Lifeless.

As if she was buried under the lava of my utterances. Had been turned to ashes by its flames. Her lips quivered, failing to say what was in her heart. Her eyes were filled with tears.

My eyes were fixed on her face.

At length, she stirred from a deep silence.

As Bachno finally returned to life, I braced myself for the words that would follow.

I felt another explosion of lava coming, the heat of which I would have to bear.

'What are you saying? I never imagined you could think this way...You are so timid...Look, my dear, I have been your life partner for two years. Tell me frankly—if I had met with an accident, lost a limb, would you have given me up? Left me?'

It took courage for her to hurl such a big question in my court.

'No! Never!' The answer freely escaped my lips.

'Then how could you think that I would leave you? Could I love anyone else? How can I leave you in the lurch? We walked around the holy fire and vowed to be life partners. Yet you now say that I should leave you. How could you think such a thing, my dear? How could you?'

Tears flowed down her cheeks; two rivers in spate.

She cried for a long while.

I did not stop her.

I wanted her to give vent to her pent-up feelings.

After some time, she calmed down.

'I wanted to understand how you felt. I did not know what was cooking in your mind. So I said what I had to. But I have hurt you…Please forgive me.'

Tears started flowing down my cheeks also.

We held each other's hands and wept for some time together, looking at each other in a strange manner.

Our eyes, which had once harboured golden dreams, mirrored nothing but sadness at present.

It is very hard to see one's dreams being shattered, but sometimes, circumstances take such a turn that, try as you will, you cannot do anything except wait for a better time; some day, your most cherished hopes might even be revived and indeed come true.

We held each other's hands tightly.

A calm began to befall us.

We smiled, radiating relief.

Our troubles were not behind us, but peace had been restored to our hearts.

'My dear, one thing is clear—we can't fill our bellies by begging. You have not lost both hands. God has blessed me with two hands, too. Can't three hands join to fill two bellies? I will work somewhere on daily wages—work as a labourer, if I must. Just remain close to me so that I feel supported by my life partner. So long as the sharer of my joys and sorrows is standing by me, no one will dare cast an evil eye on me. I should feel safe in your presence.'

Bachno was full of confidence as she looked towards the future.

'Listen, earlier, I was considered quite important in the family, and therefore so were you. But now this importance will no longer be given to us,' I replied, wiping my tears.

'Your importance will remain intact, my dear. Don't worry about that...Don't lose heart. Leave everything to God, and all will be well.'

'There is another thing. I have noticed that whenever you visit your parents, you return home crying. I know it is common among young women to weep for the family they have left behind. But our circumstances have changed. From now on, if you come back from your parental home crying, people will think it is because I am a cripple or there must not be enough food in the house.' I laid bare whatever else was on my mind.

I did not want any doubts to linger.

'My dear, I give you my word. I will not cry when I leave my parental house to return to my in-laws. I will stick to my word throughout my life,' she reassured me.

Her words were sincere.

A new energy surged within me.

We looked at one another.

In our eyes were reflected our vows to each other.

Meanwhile, the train had arrived.

Bachno boarded the train, and I returned to the hospital happy.

That night, I slept carefree like a baby.

If the mind has no burden, sleep is untroubled.

One day, when Bachno came to see me in the hospital, she looked a little unwell.

I asked the doctor to examine her. Right away, she too was admitted to the hospital and sent to the ladies' ward.

One good thing came of her sickness—we could spend a lot of time together.

Every day, we would go to the garden outside the hospital from 12 p.m. to 2 p.m. to talk.

Relatives also came almost every day to visit us. When they saw how happy we were, they were surprised. They believed we didn't care a hoot for anything. True; we were not bothered by what they thought.

We were learning how to live by His will. This is what is very difficult.

One day, the hospital received a letter from my company regarding the accident I had met with.

The hospital had been asked to conduct an inquiry into the accident. The staff divulged some of the details to me.

Soon, an army officer came to meet me. He began to inquire about the accident.

'Jawan, how did this happen to you?' he asked me.

The question put to me so suddenly hit me like a bullet.

I wondered what to say.

If I spoke the truth, the other soldier, who had given me the grenade, would be in trouble, though my accident was not through any fault of his. His only fault was that he had stolen government ammunition.

Puran Singh, you have been caught. How can you implicate a brother soldier? Think of his children. Do you want to ruin their lives? The words uttered by you can harm many lives, so weigh them carefully before you speak, I thought to myself.

When I remained quiet, the officer repeated his question.

'Sir, it was 8 a.m. I had gone out to answer the call of nature. As I was walking towards the pond for water, I spotted something round lying on the ground. I picked it up. I did not know what it was. As I was examining it, it exploded, and I lost my hand.'

The officer frowned at me.

He felt that what I had said was not true.

He was trying to read my face.

'Are you speaking the truth, young man? I think you are telling a lie,' the officer said sternly.

'Yes, sir, absolutely. Why should I lie?' I replied, now more in control of myself.

'Did this really happen the way you are saying?' he asked.

'Yes, sir, it happened the way I have explained,' I reiterated.

He repeated this question several times, and each time, I confidently gave the same reply.

Ultimately, the officer recorded my statement, obtained my signature and left.

I heaved a sigh of relief when he had gone.

I was in two minds about having fabricated the story. Was I darkening my future by telling a lie?

Was I burning my own bridge?

Why did I lie?

Why did I not reveal the truth?

I kept seeing the officer's face before my eyes, looking at me suspiciously. I turned my face this way and that, but his inquiring looks remained before me. After a while, I felt as if all the patients in the ward, along with all the nurses and doctors, were moving about bearing that officer's face.

I became terribly afraid.

I could not sleep a wink that night. And if I dozed off, the face of that officer would haunt me even in sleep.

A few days later, Bachno was discharged from the hospital and she returned to the village.

My injury had healed.

I would move about the hospital during the day.

Everyone in the ward recognized me.

Whenever anyone enquired about my arm, I related the same story that I had told the officer.

Some believed what I told them, but others did not. They would say, 'You are a soldier. Didn't you know that it was a grenade? Why did you pick it up?'

I tried my best to prove that what I had said was true.

One day, at around noon, I was lying in my bed.

Just then, two lieutenants entered our ward.

They enquired about me.

I was unnerved on hearing my name.

Someone pointed towards me.

They came up to me.

'Are you Lance Naik Puran Chand, young man?' one of them asked.

'Yes, sir, my name is Puran Chand,' I replied as I stood up and saluted them.

'We have to talk to you,' said the officer.

'Right, sir. As you order,' I said without fear.

'We will come back at 2 p.m. and take you with us to talk,' said the other officer before both of them left.

I was badly shaken once again.

I lay down in my bed.

What will they ask me now, I wondered.

The patient on the bed next to mine had heard what the officers had said to me.

After they left, he kept looking at my worried face.

He then got up and came up to me, standing by my bed.

'Dear brother, I've been watching you since the officers' departure, and it seems you are very worried. I have known you for two months—you are a courageous person; don't worry for there is no need to fear anything. Answer their questions confidently. Everything will be all right. God helps those who help themselves,' the man reassured me.

His encouragement helped calm my fears.

He appeared to me as a life raft to a drowning man.

The officers returned at 2 p.m.

With the permission of the ward-in-charge, they led me to a room.

Initially, I was worried, but then I remembered the words my fellow patient had quoted—*God helps those who help themselves*—and my resolve strengthened.

By the time we reached the room, I was in control of myself.

The officers asked me twenty-five or thirty questions.

I replied to all of them with courage.

I stuck to my stand in every reply.

'You are not as simple a person as you appear, young man. I think you are lying. Even a child could tell that the tale you are relating is a lie—just a cock and bull story,' one of the officers said angrily.

I was unnerved but soon controlled myself.

'No, sir, what I am saying is true. I am not telling a lie. Why should I?'

'Don't be scared, young man. We have been told to deal with you in this manner,' the officer said and clasped my shoulder.

They said that they would take me with them to my village at 8 a.m. the next morning and that I should be ready. With these words, they escorted me back to my ward and departed.

After they went away, another worry gripped me. What if the officers inquired about what had happened from the other villagers? If anyone in the village told them the truth, I would be nowhere. And what about the soldier who would be in trouble because of my mistake? He too would be dismissed from service.

I got terribly upset.

It as 4 p.m.

I went out of the ward.

I looked around for anyone I knew.

I wanted to send word home that I would be coming to the village, but I could spot no one.

I then quietly approached a railway worker busy at the railway crossing. I was somewhat acquainted with him. I told him that an urgent matter had come up and that he should send a message to my elder brother Babu Ram to come and meet me at the hospital gate at 9 p.m.

Upset, I returned to the ward.

My body ached.

I lay down in bed.

Scary thoughts gripped me.

Flitting between what had happened and what was likely to come, my mind abounded with questions. Although desperate to save my future, I could not wipe out the face of the other soldier from before my eyes. I felt entrapped in a web of thoughts…

Suddenly, Babu Ram appeared at my bedside. The clock had just struck 7. I felt greatly relieved on seeing him.

'What is the matter, Puran? You sent for me, and that too at this time. Is everything all right? Are you quite well?' he asked me, worried.

I related to him what had happened that day.

Urging him to go back and caution everyone in the neighbourhood, I entreated that if the officers inquired about me, they should all plead ignorance about how the accident had occurred. I also told him that cold drinks and lunch, as well as chairs and a table, should be arranged for the officers.

The next day, I waited, but the officers did not come.

Many days passed, but the officers did not return.

I had been in the hospital for two months.

The authorities there wrote to my brigade headquarters, saying that they wanted to send me to the Poona military hospital as it had better facilities than the one in Pathankot. I could be given better treatment there.

After a few days, orders were received from the brigade headquarters to send me to Poona.

I was to board the train for Poona on 25 July 1964.

It was just four or five days until I had to leave.

I was fearful that the officers would visit my village in my absence. Therefore, before leaving for Poona, I planned to go home.

I secured permission to leave the hospital for half a day before setting forth for Poona.

I boarded the train going to my village. I did not want to be seen by the village people or even by my own family. Therefore, I stealthily walked about two kilometres away from the village, into the jungle.

I wanted to fix the spot where I could say the explosion had taken place. I was uncomfortable about doing all this. To cover up one lie, I was cooking up many more, but when I thought of giving up, the face of my neighbour, the soldier, appeared before my eyes. It was for him that I was doing all this, albeit rather reluctantly.

My speaking the truth could harm him.

The only thing to be done was to come up with a credible explanation for what had happened without incriminating either of us in any wrongdoing.

A while later, I found a suitable spot.

In the evening, I stealthily walked back to the station at 5 p.m., but one of the villagers caught a glimpse of me before I could get away.

He informed my family.

They came and stopped me.

Despite my refusal, they took me home.

I did not want to face them because I felt I had done wrong. I was ashamed.

My family, however, took great care of me when I reached home.

I was served a sumptuous meal.

I told everyone to be careful to say, if they were questioned, that they were not aware of anything noteworthy about the accident.

I returned to the hospital by the evening train.

Soon, what I had feared most happened.

The next day, the two officers, along with two subedars and four or five other officers, came to the hospital in a jeep.

They had me seated in the jeep and proceeded to the village.

As we reached there, the villagers collected around us.

My elder brother Babu Ram had prepared them all to tell the same story.

The officers spoke to the villagers.

They questioned each person individually but received a universal denial of any knowledge. They came to know of the mishap after it had taken place and I had returned home, claimed the villagers.

Once the questioning was over, one of the officers asked me to lead them where the mishap had occurred.

The officers as well as my family followed me.

I took them to the spot that I had chosen the previous day.

They inspected the place.

Moved around it.

At last, fortunately, they found evidence that a military company had held a training camp in the area some time ago. They had dug trenches there. They concluded that since a training camp had been organized there, some explosives might have been left behind by mistake. When they asked me why there were no bloodstains near the site, one of the officers said that the mishap had occurred many days earlier. The stains had probably been washed away by the rains.

One of the subedars drew a map of the scene of the accident, citing the likelihood of a military training camp having been held there.

'It appears to us that this young man is not speaking the truth. Advise him to tell us what really happened. He will be paid a tidy sum,' whispered a lieutenant as he took the village lambardar aside.

The headman drew near me to convey the offer.

Many questions arose in my mind when I heard about the reward, but the face of the innocent soldier appeared before me again.

'Sir, treasures can be exhausted, but honour can't be bought at any price. I have told you the truth,' I replied.

The lambardar patted my back.

He informed the officer of my response, who appeared to be somewhat disappointed.

Evcrybody returned to the village.

On the way, one of the subedars took me to one side and said, 'Just tell me the truth, Puran. I will not disclose it to anyone, I will keep it to myself.'

I repeated the same: 'Sir, I have spoken the truth. Why are you pressing me to tell a lie?'

On reaching the village, the officers put down in writing the entire proceedings, which were read out to the people of the village. The worthies of the village affixed their signatures to the document as witnesses.

The officers then brought me back to the hospital.

'Puran Chand, I helped you a lot, but you did not speak the truth,' a lieutenant later said to me as we were standing in the verandah.

'If that is so, sir, then write down that when I returned home on leave, I had some hand grenades stashed in my luggage. That having gathered a crowd, I was showing the villagers how to use the grenades when this explosion took place, blowing my hand off. Write that down, sir. Are you happy now?' I said rather resentfully.

The officer yielded.

He handed me over to the ward-in-charge and left the hospital premises.

I heaved a sigh of relief because I had passed the first examination.

Life tests you all the time. On some occasions, we fail, and on others, we succeed. But sometimes, the fruit of our efforts cannot be discerned immediately.

The next day, I boarded the train for Poona.

Arriving in the city two days later, I headed straight for the Poona military hospital and submitted my papers.

Once admitted, I relaxed there for some days.

But what sort of relaxation was it really? The question of what would happen to me in the future weighed heavily on my mind. I had a feeling that I would perhaps not be entitled to a pension.

In fact, according to military regulations of the time, a soldier who had been in service for less than ten years would not be entitled to a pension if he lost a limb in an accident while on leave. If he died, however, under similar circumstances, his dependents had to be paid a pension. Since I had served only eight years, I was unlikely to qualify for a pension. How would I then spend the rest of my life? I often started crying thinking of this.

A few days later, another wounded soldier, a Sikh man, was admitted. Both his legs had been severed in a rail accident. The government had decided not to pay him a pension because he, too, had met with the accident while he was on leave.

In spite of this, he always looked cheerful and would repeat his prayer of gratitude over and over:

Thy will is sweet,
Thy Name is all that I seek, Nanak.

His company encouraged me a lot.

He always told me to remain in high spirits. He often tried to explain the teachings of Gurbani to me.

'Look here, brother Puran, happiness and unhappiness are nothing but one's state of mind, which alters as often as the weather. Both are merely two aspects of the same thing and can't be fully uncoupled from one another. Without unhappiness, happiness cannot be found, and without happiness, unhappiness cannot be understood. In fact, the absence of happiness is called unhappiness. As man is connected to the body, he regards physical and material happiness as the perfect happiness and constantly hankers after it. Because of man's dependence on outer conditions and worldly objects for his happiness, as the outside world changes according to the laws of nature, so do man's joys and sorrows.

'Dear Puran, that is why the human mind is always dithering and is unable to attain eternal happiness. It is only an illusion in the mind of man that the cause of joy or sorrow lies outside; the real cause of sorrow is the lack of understanding within. Because of a lack of understanding, gripped by evil, we embrace miseries. To get rid of them and enjoy eternal peace, we will have to give up our evil ways and seek shelter in God.

'The True Emperor has Himself written down the joys and sorrows. Our love for material objects has also been ordained by God. When His laws cannot be changed, praying for bodily comforts, yearning and lamenting, is a useless pursuit. Misfortunes happen to everyone; ask anyone, Puran Chand.

'Tell anyone of your misery, dear Puran Chand, and you will find that they too are full of their own miseries. They will begin to relate their own tale of woes. The great saint Baba Farid has said that he thought it was only he who was miserable, but when he looked around, he found that the whole world was miserable. Because this is the law of nature. Because of these outer miseries, man tries to seek happiness. He does this through meditation, concentration, prayers, worship, the reciting of hymns and other deeds but in vain.

'Dear brother Puran, Baba Farid says that joys and sorrows should be considered alike and evil thrown out of your mind. Live in His will. Regard it as the best for you. And you will reach the Kingdom of God. Accepting all joys and sorrows is living in His will. And living in his will, being free of evil, weeds out unhappiness, leaving behind only happiness.

'Therefore, brother Puran, there is no use weeping. No gain at all.

'Only he knows the essence of life who considers joy and sorrow, respect and disrespect, happiness and unhappiness, all, to be alike. He remains free of desire. But it is a very difficult path to follow, and rarely can one understand it. One who follows the path shown by the Guru and is freed of evil can understand the mystery of life and passes the difficult test to attain eternal joy.'

Truly speaking, the company of the soldier encouraged me quite a lot.

He was, no doubt, a saintly person.

A few days later, the hospital assigned me the duty of going to the workshop where my artificial hand was to be made.

I began going there every day. The workers there measured my other hand carefully.

It took them eight or nine days to get the measurements right.

In the evening, I would roam about Poona.

I visited many important places.

I also saw many patients in the hospital; one of them had lost both his legs.

One had only one arm; he had lost two legs and one arm.

There was another patient whose legs had been amputated till right above the knees.

He went on duty daily using artificial legs. In the evening, he removed the prostheses. It was horrifying to look at him.

I felt relieved when I saw that I had not lost as much as others.

Both my legs were intact. One arm was complete.

One day, two surgeons came to see me.

'Puran Chand, we want to conduct a 'cooking work operation' on your arm,' they said.

'What is that?' I asked.

'We will divide the stump of your left hand into two parts such that they can work like two fingers, helping you do your work.'

They tried to explain what they were planning to do, but I could not make sense of it.

They wanted me to understand how the operation would modify my hand, how it would work, and what it would look like. So they asked me to meet a Gorkha soldier.

They wanted me to give my consent to the operation only after I had seen him.

I met the soldier.

I had a look at his arm, on which the doctors had performed the same operation that they were planning for me.

I liked what I saw.

The next day, I gave my consent to the doctors.

The doctors assigned me the date of the operation.

I wrote to my family, informing them about my operation.

After a few days, I received a reply that as they were too far away to judge the situation, I should do what I thought best.

On the appointed date, the operation began at noon and ended at 3 p.m.

Afterwards, I was sent back to my ward.

The doctors heaved a sigh of relief at the success of the operation.

I regained consciousness at about 4 p.m., but I felt such severe pain that even the noise made by the ceiling fan aggravated my distress.

They gave me a sleeping pill and some painkillers.

That night, a civilian came to my bed.

On account of his severed leg, he had got an artificial leg made. He encouraged me quite a lot.

Over the next two months, I spent a lot of time with him.

I became quite close to him. I liked his nature. He, too, was from a poor family. He hailed from near Jammu.

One day, he came to me looking crestfallen.

I asked him what was wrong, but he kept quiet.

When I persisted, he began his tale of woe.

'Dear brother Puran, you know that I belong to a village near Jammu. We have been together for over two months. I go back home tomorrow, by the 6 a.m. train. But brother Puran, I only have enough money to pay for the fare up to Delhi. So I will stay there for a few days. I will beg so that I can collect some money. Only then will I be able to go to Jammu. Earlier, my leg gave me a lot of trouble, but this new leg is all right, I am able to walk now. It will shame me to beg, but there is no other way. On reaching Jammu, I will try to do some work in the village and begin my life all over again.' He broke into tears.

I thought that I should help this man.

I put my hand under my pillow and pulled out a five-rupee note.

That was all the money I had.

I tried to hand him the note, but he would not accept it. Finally, I forcibly put it into his pocket.

He thanked me profusely, and the tears kept flowing down his cheeks.

I felt better after helping him.

I experienced great peace of mind.

It was the first sound sleep I had had in several nights.

At noon the next day, someone told me that the postman was waiting for me outside.

I wondered what he wanted with me.

I went out to him.

'Are you Puran Chand?' he asked.

'Yes, sir, I am. What can I do for you?' I showed him my ID card.

'Here is a money order in your name for five hundred rupees,' said the postman.

'Five hundred rupees? Who has sent it? From where?' I was stunned.

Who could have sent me a money order for five hundred rupees?

How had this miracle happened?

'It is from your company in Roorkee. They have sent you a message also,' said the postman.

I received the money order from him.

Then I read the message that had been sent with it.

It said that many jawans of our company had contributed money and they had managed to collect five hundred rupees for me, which they were sending by money order. It was also written that perhaps I would not be entitled to a pension.

I was shocked to hear that I was not entitled to a pension but I controlled my emotions.

I gave the postman ten rupees out of the five hundred rupees.

He was very glad to receive the money.

He showered blessings upon me.

I felt that this miracle was His work, who is high above.

I had donated only five rupees last night, and He had sent me five hundred!

I thanked God for this bounty.

This amount of five hundred rupees encouraged me very much.

After a few days, the hospital in Poona received a letter from the Roorkee centre saying that if my operation had been successful and the wound healed, I should be sent back.

While the hospital prepared my medical certificate, my artificial hand was being readied at the workshop.

They gave me two such hands and certain other tools that I could use to attend to various domestic chores. Such as a sickle for cutting grass. A hook for lifting loads. A set of fingers with the help of which I could type.

All these things were put into a toolbox and handed to me.

Next, I had an interview with the chief manager of the hospital.

Describing my challenging circumstances, I told him that I was not entitled to receive a pension. I requested him to help me find a job somewhere. He said that he would write to various departments on my behalf.

'We can try another thing also—you can write an application stating that you are alone and have no sister, brother, wife, children, etc., and therefore should be helped financially. This should fetch you about fifteen thousand rupees,' suggested the chief manager.

It was an odd suggestion that was difficult to follow. He was trying to help me, but how could I say that I had no family? Thinking of this, the faces of my family members appeared before my eyes.

'Sir, I have brothers, sisters and a mother. A wife too. How can I write that I have no one? If you can help me get something from the government, well and good. But I won't write any lies if you can't,' I told the manager plainly.

He was happy to hear my views but responded that he could not help me in any other manner.

Nonetheless, I was hopeful of finding a job somewhere.

On 21 January 1965, I left Poona for Roorkee.

I reached Roorkee three days later.

I showed up at the Record Office.

They settled my accounts.

It was confirmed there that I would not be paid a pension.

My discharge certificate was prepared, and I was relieved of my service.

There was no farewell gathering. Only a few friends were present.

I thought about how soldiers were always ready to lay down their lives to protect the country. A soldier left his home and hearth and fought battles for the country, but if he lost a limb, he was declared an invalid and relieved, without even a pension to save him from running from pillar to post to survive.

I thought, when a soldier is on leave, is he not in the service of the government?

Is he not paid a salary for the period of his leave?

And if he is crippled in an accident, is he at fault? The only fault on his part is that he decided to enrol in the army to serve the country.

Is this the price of patriotism?

The reward for his sacrifices?

Is it fair?

But the only answer anyone had was that things had to be done according to the law.

Luck had played with me a strange game.

After nearly nine months of treatment, I was reborn as another person. Earlier, I was serving in the army in fine health—laughing, playing games, working—and, now, suddenly I was rendered an invalid. Helpless. As long as I lived, I would have to struggle to earn my livelihood. This suffocating feeling of apprehension was constantly on my mind.

One of the majors at the Roorkee centre—a Major Vohra—was a very good person. I told him about myself and my family. I requested him to help me find a job. He immediately drove me to the Employment Exchange in his jeep. My name was registered there. A card was issued to me. That evening, when we returned to the Roorkee centre, Major Vohra said that from Monday onwards, I should start working as a peon in the office.

It was a Friday.

I told Major Vohra that I wanted to go home for a couple of days and would join duty on Monday.

He agreed.

I boarded the train for my village.

Once at home, I told my family about my time in Poona and Roorkee.

I discussed everything with my wife as well.

She told me to do what I thought best.

What else could my family do?

They could only sympathize with me.

Bachno was very quiet but tried to seem carefree rather than burdened in her silence. Her heart was intent on boosting my self-confidence. Though she might be crying within, she put on a happy face in my presence.

I understood what she was feeling.

Many thoughts began to weigh heavily on my mind.

I thought if I worked as a peon at the Roorkee centre, I would have to rent a house. I would have to cook my own food. How would I cook my food with one hand? If I ate food in the government mess, what would I save? There, I would worry about home also.

Whenever I met my old friends at the centre, looking at them in uniform, how would I feel? I would find it difficult to face them. The atmosphere there would make my life hell. I would fall in my own estimation.

Then I thought, *if I have to work as a peon, why do so at Roorkee necessarily?*

Why at my own centre?

After lots of deliberation, I decided not to go back to Roorkee.

I wrote a letter to Major Vohra.

I sought his forgiveness.

I made up my mind to find a job near my village.

I went out in search of work, carrying with me the recommendation written by the head of the military hospital.

First, I went to the Ferozpur railway headquarters.

I applied for a Class IV position there, which included vacancies for a water man and other odd jobs.

They called me on 15 March to the main office in Pathankot.

I reported there, but they sent me back and told me to return on another date.

The next day, I went to the District Employment Office. I submitted an application but in vain.

I went to the nearby schools as well.

A headmaster told me that his regular peon had gone on leave, and I could work while he was away if I wanted. But when he realized that I was one-handed, he changed his mind.

I went to many other offices also.

I tried very hard to find a job.

But it was to no avail.

I revisited the railway office in Pathankot but had no luck there once again.

Meanwhile, my elder brother had arranged the marriage of his son, Chunni Lal. I was responsible for some of the duties related to the wedding because I had no kids of my own yet. The children of Charan Das and Punjab Das were very young.

I wanted my grown-up nephews and nieces to be married while we were all living as a joint family.

I was held in high esteem in the house. The family agreed to all my counsel. I wanted my elder brother to lighten his burden by continuing to live in the joint family.

Chunni Lal was married to a girl from a village near Dhariwal.

Banso, my elder brother's daughter, was married to a boy from a nearby village.

I had not yet found a job.

I repented giving up the job I had been offered at Roorkee.

One day, it occurred to me that I should try to get a job at the GREF office at Pathankot. I had gone there during my first annual leave to get my elder brother Charan Das recruited there.

He had gotten a job, thanks to my efforts.

I went to the office the following day.

I met the colonel there.

He took pity on me.

He hired me as a peon.

I had won for the second time.

I was at peace.

The next stage of the journey of my life was about to begin.

I resolved not to accept defeat.

Come what may, I would live with honour and die with honour.

Five

5 July 1965 was the first day of my service as a peon in GREF.

I cycled to Pathankot—it took me one and a half hours.

The first day was quite hard. I felt a bit small, but I had nowhere else to go. I filled a glass of water with one hand and served it to my boss on a plate.

When he rang the bell, I had to appear before him.

I cycled for an hour and a half again to return home in the evening.

After three or four days, I was exhausted.

Cycling such a long distance every day was getting very difficult.

So, for a few days, I moved in with a relative who lived alone in Pathankot.

He worked as a tailor and he had rented a shop.

I ate my meals at a dhaba and spent the nights at my relative's place. The owner of the dhaba charged me thirty rupees per month. He served me three meals a day. In the morning, he gave me two parathas. In the afternoon and evening, he gave me one dal and one sabzi and six thin chapattis.

The chapattis were not sufficient to satiate my hunger. My companions could make do, no doubt, but I remained hungry.

One day, an elderly sardar asked the dhaba owner for another chapatti. He humiliated him badly.

Though I too wanted another, I did not ask for it.

After a month, I stopped eating at the dhaba.

I rented a room for ten rupees in a village near the office.

I brought Bachno to live with me.

Life became easy for me.

I would cycle to the office.

I ate at home and to my heart's content.

During one of her following visits to her parents' house, she learnt how to stitch clothes.

Bachno then began to make garments for the villagers.

We would go to our own village every Saturday.

My elder brothers were planning to live separately. But they were afraid of what I would say. They also feared people would say that because their younger brother had been crippled, they had made him leave the house. This worried me quite a lot, too.

In those days, Punjab Das lived in the railway quarters in Dina Nagar.

The next time we went to our village, I told my brothers and their wives to ask Punjab Das to come home the following Saturday.

'We will make preparations to live separately. But don't disclose this to the people in the village. They will scoff at us,' I told my family.

A week later, we went back. Punjab Das had also come. Charan Das was at home on leave.

We had our dinner together.

All of us four brothers were closeted in a room.

We waited for our neighbours to go to sleep.

Late at night, we began the process of separation.

Everything was divided with the consent of all.

This included rooms, jewellery, grain, cots, bedding, etc.

I decided that Bebe would stay with me.

We finally went to sleep at 2 a.m.

In the morning, all of us left for work.

Days passed as time went on at its own pace.

On Sunday, 3 April 1966, at about 11 a.m., while living in the village Dhira, we were blessed with a son.

The first thing we did was to check whether both his hands were all right.

When we found that he was *complete*, we were very relieved.

Bachno had been worried all along that the baby to be born might be without a limb.

She was extremely happy on finding her son with all his limbs intact.

Her heart was dancing with happiness.

We saw our future reflected in our newborn.

On seeing him, I felt as if my severed hand had been returned to me.

When the time came to bestow a name on the boy, I called him Govardhan Prasad. His nickname was Gabbi. Later, his name was changed to Govardhan Lal in school.

Years ago, when I was serving in Roorkee, there was an officer there named Govardhan Prasad. I had made up my mind at that time that if I had a son, I would call him by this name. He too would be a big man one day.

While I felt happy looking at our child, the seeds of another worry had been sown, which weighed heavily on my mind. It was my salary that was causing me concern. I was being paid only one hundred rupees. I had to pay the rent as well as purchase provisions for the household. It was difficult to make the money last till the end of the month. Sometimes, I had to borrow from my colleagues to meet my expenses. I disliked this very much.

How would we bring up our child in such circumstances?

Both of us worried about this all the time.

We did not want to rear our child in poverty.

Therefore, the question of how I could earn more money dominated my thoughts.

Both of us tried to devise ways and means to earn more.

Above all, we decided that I should leave my current job as my salary was only one hundred rupees. But then what would I do once I gave up the job?

How would I increase my incomc?

I could not get a higher-paying job.

This war continued within me for many days.

Ultimately, on 30 September 1966, I resigned.

Then, I wondered what I should do.

I deliberated for many days.

At last, I decided to open a retail shop. But where?

That was another big question.

My in-laws were good people. They sympathized with me. They wanted to help me in my difficult times.

I talked to them. They were ready to stand by me.

I decided to open a shop in my in-laws' village.

Two or three days after quitting my job, we went to their village.

Soon, I was able to open the shop.

I had saved some money. The rest was given by my in-laws. I stocked the shop quite well.

The shop did good business.

The daily sale amounted to forty or fifty rupees.

I was very happy with this.

I felt that leaving my job had not been a mistake.

There was a newly calved cow at my in-laws' house.

Our child got enough milk to fill his belly.

I would wake up at 5 a.m. every day and cycle to the nearby vegetable market to purchase vegetables and other necessities.

The shop was running well.

We were quite happy and content.

This happiness did not last long.

Just a month after I had opened the shop, another person in the village opened a shop opposite mine.

With the opening of his shop, my sales dropped.

I began to run into losses.

The new shop owner would also loudly taunt me that there was no difference between a man staying at his in-laws' house and a dog.

After some time, I too felt that he was right.

Bachno too seemed to be worried all the time.

She had not been in favour of my plan but had not said so openly. She had wanted me to open a shop anywhere except in her parents' village.

I ran the shop for about two months. Ultimately, I got fed up.

I sold my stock to the other shopkeeper.

He was very happy.

He had won.

Life had once again struck me down, but I would try to stand back up on my feet.

I thought of opening a shop in some other village.

I tried but could not find a suitable place.

When I did the final accounts, I realized that I had suffered a loss of about one hundred and fifty rupees.

Again, I began to worry constantly.

I had set out to improve our situation but ended up worsening it.

This happens in life. Man proposes. God disposes.

God once again appeared to be unhappy with me.

It seemed as if He wanted me to be heated in a melting pot to turn me into pure gold.

I too made up my mind to pass through the melting pot to become pure.

Ultimately, I returned to my own village with my wife and child.

Two days before our departure, I met a person who bought plastic and rubber chappals and shoes from elsewhere and hawked them in villages. He told me that it was a good business.

A few days after we had moved back to my village, I returned to my in-laws' place.

I met that man again.

He told me that he and his partners were going to Jalandhar the following Saturday to purchase footwear. I could accompany them if I desired.

The next Saturday, I set out with my new acquaintances with two hundred rupees in my wallet.

I also made purchases with them.

I bought whatever they bought.

We had our meal in the evening.

To pass the time, I went to two movies with them.

After that, we went to the railway station with bags full of goods.

We spent the night sprawled on the platform, waiting for the passenger train that ran from Jalandhar to Pathankot. It departed early in the morning.

At dawn, we loaded our bags on to the train.

The men got down at my in-laws' village.

Around noon, I alighted at my village station.

Once home, I put away my purchases safely.

I thought about going out for a round of selling but could not overcome a certain hesitation in the pit of my stomach.

I felt a little ashamed.

Ultimately, I stayed put at home.

Four or five days passed in this way.

Since my return from Jalandhar, I had become a bit short-tempered.

Unhappy with my new attitude, Bachno was turning wary of me.

One day, she requested an elderly shopkeeper in the village to advise me that if I had bought footwear to sell, I should pluck up the courage to go ahead and do it.

The next day, while everyone was away attending a wedding, the shopkeeper dropped in to speak to me.

'Who do you think you are, Puran? Are you a VIP? Hmm...the rope is burnt but its knots are not loosened. What accounts for your pride that you won't deign to sell your goods? What do you have? Nothing? Then what are you afraid of? Shame? The boys who come to our village on their cycles to sell clothes do not feel ashamed. They wear hundred-rupee suits. Are you a duke of some princely state? You are a little boy's father—responsible for his well-being. You have spent good money to buy chappals and shoes, yet you remain in hiding, confined to the house twenty-four hours like an idler. Get up and show courage, my son. Put the chappals and shoes in a box and go for a round. God will help you.' The old man both chastised and motivated me.

At length, I stood up.

Stuffing a box with a variety of footwear, I strapped it to the carrier of my cycle.

I tied some chappals and shoes together on a string and suspended them from the handlebar.

With a nervous but determined spirit, I then stepped out.

I went where the road took me.

Suddenly, I found myself in a nearby village.

A girl saw the chappals dangling from my handlebar.

'Are these for sale, brother?' she asked.

'Yes, sister.' The words escaped my lips with difficulty.

The girl smiled a little.

She called her friends to her side.

All the girls surrounded my cycle and looked at the chappals.

They asked me the price.

As the men I had travelled to Jalandhar with had told me to ask for more than the cost price, I quoted three rupees and fifty paisa for a chappal purchased for one and a half rupees.

'That is too much...reduce it. We will pay you three rupees for a pair, and we will buy all the chappals,' said one of the girls.

'Though I will make no profit, I will give you the chappals at that rate,' I replied and felt pleased with myself.

Instead of one pair, all of them bought two each.

I pocketed the money and went to another lane.

Here, too, a girl called out to me, others in the mohalla soon collecting around my cycle.

I had a brisk sale.

In the evening, I returned home.

My family hadn't returned from the wedding yet.

I was very happy.

The sales from that day had amounted to sixty rupees.

About thirty rupees of that was my profit.

I recalled that when I was doing night guard duty in the past, I was being paid forty rupees a month as the salary. Today, I had earned thirty rupees in one day.

As soon as the family returned, I told Bachno about the profit. This made her very happy.

I placed all the money before her.

She counted it and was greatly pleased.

She moved around the house with quick, happy steps, as if she were dancing.

She thanked God.

The next day, I took a round of another village. The sales were as good as they had been the previous day.

I returned home in the evening.

Bachno was very elated.

This continued.

I would go to Jalandhar to purchase goods three or four times a month.

I had become very familiar with the wholesalers.

Sometimes, goods that I had purchased for a hundred rupees fetched me five hundred rupees.

A while later, I began to buy goods from the factory directly. This proved to be even more profitable.

I became familiar to the residents in various villagers as a shoe hawker.

There were other hawkers who too sold chappals, but I had regular customers.

Once again, I had succeeded in bringing my life back on track.

A new routine had crystallized.

I said my prayers in the morning.

Got ready.

Had my breakfast and left to make rounds of the nearby villages on my cycle.

Bachno took care of the house.

We had a cow.

Bachno would bring fodder for it and clean out the dung.

On 31 December 1968, our second son was born.

We named him Sarwan.

Life was good.

The children were growing up.

Our hopes and aspirations were rising.

The maize crop was ripening in the fields.

One day, my elder son, who was about six years old at that time, came home crying.

When we asked him what the matter was, he said that he had gone to a farmer's field to cut grass.

Along with grass, he had plucked a ripe cob also. The farmer had slapped him and taken the cob as well as the grass from him.

When he told us this, we felt very upset. But what could we do?

We could not go and pick a quarrel with the farmer.

Both of us swore that day that our son would not go to anyone's field for grass.

He would either to go to our own field (whenever God blessed us with one) or not at all.

Around the same time, we began to save five to ten rupees a day. By 1972, we had with us about three thousand rupees.

We were on the lookout for a piece of land.

Luckily, we found an acre to purchase.

It was not irrigated, but we hoped it would yield grass and fodder. We bought this land.

We began farming it.

In due course, the land began supplementing our income.

We were also blessed with a daughter.

We named her Sumitri.

Meanwhile, the nearby landowners began dropping by our house when news spread that "the hawker" was buying some land.

I started paying one or two of the landowners monthly instalments towards the price of the land. I also sold them chappals on credit.

In this way, in a couple of years' time, we had bought about five acres of land.

We had become landlords.

Those who had sold us their lands ploughed the fields and did the sowing for us.

After some time, I told them that I would till my own land.

We now took up farming by ourselves.

We bought a pair of bullocks for five hundred rupees, in addition to plough and a leveller.

By 1976, we had five children—two sons and three daughters. The daughters born after Sumitri were named Seema and Sunita.

The family had a daily schedule.

I got up early and went to the fields.

Ploughed the land.

Cut grass for the cattle.

Returned home by around 9 a.m.

Had my bath and breakfast; then went out for a hawking round.

Bachno looked after the children.

She fed the cattle grass and fodder.

The children had begun to go to school.

After they returned from school, they went to the fields.

We had built a small shed where we kept our farming implements.

In those days, there was a shortage of drinking water.

We started digging a well in a corner of the land.

We dug every day from 4 p.m. to 6 p.m.

Both my sons joined me in the endeavor.

The three of us were able to sink the well in fifteen days.

We raised a loan of five thousand rupees from the bank.

The well was bricked.

Now we could draw cold drinking water from our own well.

We also kept a rope and a bucket at the well for passers-by so that no one who came to our well went away thirsty.

Every day, I got up as the cock crowed and awakened my sons with a song:

Get up my sons
Enter the field
Do something and
Show me
What is to be done
I will tell you.
Come and
Just follow me.

One sleeps deeply in the small hours. My sons would not want to get up. They would press their palms on their eyes.

They stretched.

They yawned and huddled under the sheets. When I reprimanded them, they reluctantly got up.

Taking water from the pitcher kept on a stand, they washed up.

Once ready, each of us would wrap a *khes* around the shoulders, the light blanket protecting us from the chilly morning air.

As we tied a kerchief around our heads, on which to place baskets of dung and rubbish, I would resume singing:

The same path but two things to do

Both the brothers responded in unison:

Carry chaff on return, dung as we go

At that time, ours was an arid region.

Farming depended on the rains.

I ploughed the fields. The children broke the big lumps of earth with pestles.

I would sing to the bullocks at the turning of a furrow:

Ho, ho, ho, ho, ho
Move ahead, move ahead
You handsome, sweet ones
No one can rival you

The bullocks swung their tails and drew a line on the chest of the earth with the plough before reaching the other end.

I would sing loudly as I laboured hard in the fields:

Sassi and Punnu were two of them
They held a red handkerchief in their hands
The great God had written their fate
Which no one can avert

O Punnu, you cruel one
You are my soulmate
Don't go away leaving me alone

When I spotted Bachno in the distance, carrying our breakfast, my voice and gait would quicken.

I would bow before the food, look towards the sky, touch the earth and strew some fragments of chapatti for the birds.

Before putting the first morsel in my mouth, I would repeat a couplet from a solemn hymn:

Thou art the bountiful Lord and
We partake of what Thou gives us

Bachno would bring two thick chapattis or big balls of dough for the bullocks also.

That is why when the bullocks saw her, they felt happy at the prospect of getting both some food and rest.

As they swung their tails and walked, the bells around their necks played music of many kinds.

When I used the leveller after ploughing, Gabbi and Shabha would jump on it and sing:

The friends' truck is going
Get into it quietly...

Every day, I would go around villages to sell chappals.

On my way back home in the evening, I would buy from the country liquor vendor a small glass or two and croon a film song:

Have no desire
No aspiration
What is my life?
A cut-thread kite

On the unmanned railway crossing outside the village, both my sons would wait for me to help me drag the box of chappals and the cycle laden with bags over the rail tracks.

I perceived my golden future in both my sons.

As I saw them waiting for me, I would hum:

The queen of my dreams
When will you come?
Heady weather has come
When will you come?
Life is passing by
When will you come?
Come hither
Come hither….

At home, Bachno would welcome me with a smile before I broke into another song:

I put scarf around my neck
And pray for your happiness
If I could meet you alone
I could relate my tale of woes

I had learnt by heart a *qissa* by the poet Kali Das. I was fond of this particular folk tale because like its main character, I too was named Puran and was without one hand.

Sometimes, while relating this tale, when I reached the point where Queen Loona complains to King Salwan, under whose orders the executioner severs both of Puran's hands, the atmosphere would turn sad. I would sing the gut-wrenching lines with a heavy heart:

The cruel executioner wielded his sword
And severed both his hands and feet then
So much blood was shed, the earth turned red
As a canal broke its banks and overflowed

Tears would flow down my cheeks.
My family would also started sobbing.

Days turned to months and months to years.

At the time of sowing and harvesting, my father-in-law would come to our village. He helped us quite a lot.

One year, the rains had been scanty.

The crops did not grow.

I thought of doing something else.

We decided to plant an orange orchard because in a nearby village, an orchard was leased on a contract basis for five to six thousand rupees every year.

The following day, we got orange and guava saplings from Pathankot.

We planted the saplings on three acres of land.

The plants grew.

They began to bear fruit.

We also planted eucalyptus trees on the periphery of the fields.

The oranges ripened in winter.

In the mornings, we plucked the oranges and gathered them in baskets.

Following this, I went out for a round to sell chappals.

Around 8 p.m. at night, we loaded a tonga with baskets of oranges and drove to GT Road.

From there, we took the produce by truck to the market.

Sometimes, we went to Jalandhar; other times, to Ludhiana and Chandigarh.

We traversed the entire journey wrapped in a blanket or a shawl, given that it was winter and we were riding in an open truck.

We reached the market in the morning.

Sold the oranges and returned.

Soon, the harvesting of paddy would start.

After threshing the rice at night, we slept in the fields, keeping watch over the crop until morning.

We were cold and scared but determined to stay put.

This continued throughout the winter season.

Sowing paddy was always a difficult business.

We had to irrigate the fields at night.

By then, tube wells had come up in our area.

Water was supplied to the farmers in turns.

Sometimes, our turn came at night.

At the time, the children were very young.

So I'd fetch the water alone, often encountering snakes along the way. Sometimes, an insect or creeper would sting me.

I also ensured that the water supplied to us was not diverted to other fields. Though, sometimes, our water seeped into other fields through rat holes.

The tube well was located at some distance from our fields.

Occasionally, there was a power breakdown at night, and I had to go to the tube well to restart it.

Wrapping myself in a shawl, I would pick up a spade and keep it over my shoulder as I moved through the jungle to start the motor.

To my mind, there is hardly anyone who does not love their place of birth. Who does not treasure the memories of such a beloved land? Who does not often recall the days spent there? Who does not dream about their birthplace? Who does not imagine flowers blooming in their native village? If some calamity befalls their motherland, who is not pained? Who can stop the tears flowing from their eyes?

As I went through life, my place of birth in Pakistan was always on my mind.

It is not only us human beings who cherish such memories. Even birds and animals love their motherland—perhaps even more than their lives. I had read somewhere that tortoises, who live their entire lives in water, desire to return to the shore where they were born.

I remember when the children were young, we had kept a dog in our house. We called him Dabbu. His mother had been run over by a train, dying a few days after he was born. As we reared him, the pup became an integral part of our house. He remained ever ready to serve us. He played with us the whole day. When we went to the fields, he followed us. He ran after the cattle to herd them. If we had to go out at night to answer the call of nature, he accompanied us. As he grew, we felt safe in his company.

One day, he fell sick. He could not tell us what ailed him, and we could not know what it was. He remained unwell and inert for quite a while, dozing under the cot the whole day. When we left the house, he did not stir as he used to in the past. The children tried to force him to get up and follow them. They teased him with a lash. He protested once or twice by barking a little, but they paid no heed. When they continued to irritate him, he retaliated more aggressively, ending up biting my younger son.

The boy had to be taken to the doctor.

He had to be given injections.

That day, I thrashed Dabbu.

Abused him.

'Run away from here! We will not keep you with us. You bite those in whose house you live and eat. Don't you feel ashamed?' I cursed him.

Dabbu was feeling deeply guilty, no doubt.

He wagged his tail, stood with his head lowered and listened to me. He was lamenting like a child seeking forgiveness. When I continued to shout at him, he left the house but returned in the evening and went to sleep under the cot.

I flew into a rage again when I saw him back in the house.

I did not rebuke him again, as suggested by the children, but I made up my mind that the dog would not remain in the house.

By chance, the children's maternal uncle had come to visit us. I suggested that he take the dog with him. Else, he would not leave us. The next day, he put the dog into a gunny bag and took him along on the train journey back to his village, which was twenty-five to thirty miles away. He had made a few holes in the bag so that the dog could see through them and breathe in fresh air. The bag was necessary because such animals were not allowed on the train.

I was happy that Dabbu was gone, but the children missed him very much.

He had been away for only three or four days when I saw him lying asleep under the cot.

As soon as he saw us, he thrust his tail between his hind legs and began to lick my and the children's legs. He joyously ran around us in circles, coming up to me and Bachno in turns. He lay down on his back and then jumped up again and again. Still ill, tears clouded his eyes. Was he happy or in pain? I could not tell.

Why don't you reason with Papa? Why don't you tell him anyone can be in the wrong? Such a big punishment for such a small mistake...I was separated from my birthplace. I pray to you in the name of God: don't send me away again, he appeared to be saying to the children.

His love, affection and lamentations won me over. I agreed to take him back.

The children were very happy.

But his condition worsened with every passing day. He had already been sick. Then, he had travelled such a long distance, only to return home. My father-in-law told us that he had not eaten anything while he was with them. They had put a collar around his neck to keep him in the house. He had cried the whole day.

Concerned, we took him to a doctor for treatment. The medication continued for quite some time, but we remained helpless in the face of the ailment he had.

After a while, Dabbu departed, leaving us behind forever. All of us wept over his passing away. Deeply remorseful, we felt responsible for his death. If we had not sent him away, he would not have fallen ill, suffering the pangs of separation from his place of birth. He may not have died so soon. Even today, when I think of Dabbu, my eyes well up with hot tears.

The children were now in middle and primary schools.

Expenses had increased.

I had to work harder.

I continued farming the land.

Tended the orchard too.

Went on rounds to sell chappals as well.

To earn more from hawking, I went to distant villages.

When both our sons returned from school, we sent them to the neighbouring villages to sell vegetables and guavas.

A basket containing the produce was tied to the carrier of the cycle.

The boys would place their cycle against a tree and set up a stall on the ground under its shade.

They never went from lane to lane hawking like other vegetable sellers.

They did not have the courage to open their mouths and hawk loudly.

The village women would come to them asking about what they were selling.

Some of their classmates lived in those villages.

The kids told the others in the class that the boys had come to their village to sell vegetables. Because of this revelation, our sons started to suffer from a sort of inferiority complex.

They began to lag behind in their studies.

When I came to know about this, we realized what the problem was.

We stopped sending them to sell vegetables.

In those days, the farmers in our village were poor.

I used to help many of them.

I loaned them money and sold chappals and shoes on credit.

When they harvested their crops, they repaid the loan or the amount they owed for buying on credit.

In 1985, our elder son passed his twelfth class and went to Jammu to study engineering.

Our other children also moved up to higher classes.

Expenses increased all the more.

Bachno and I tried to work harder still.

Six

While he was still enrolled in college, our elder son Govardhan began tutoring younger students to supplement our domestic income.

Soon after, our younger son was admitted to Sanatan Dharma College in Pathankot.

He would leave around 6 a.m. every morning, carrying with him oranges, guavas, tomatoes, etc., to the vegetable market to sell them before going to college.

The financial contributions of both our sons proved very important to us.

Four years later, Govardhan became a civil engineer.

We were very happy.

We felt as if it was our first victory.

He went to Chandigarh in search of a job.

He served for a year and then opened a coaching centre in partnership with a classmate.

Our second son, Sarwan, wanted to become a doctor and secured admission in a medical college in Ludhiana.

Sumitri went to Bhatinda to study architecture, and Seema went to study electronics at Hoshiarpur Polytechnic.

Sunita went to stay with her brother in Chandigarh and enrolled in a bachelor's course.

Our elder son had taken upon himself the responsibility of meeting both their expenses.

Eventually, we arranged Govardhan's marriage.

A few years later, our eldest daughter Sumitri too tied the knot.

The respective weddings of Seema, Dr Sarwan and Sunita followed in due course.

Now, Bachno and I are living in Chandigarh with both our sons and their families.

Initially, we did not feel at home in Chandigarh, but now we are quite used to it. We are very happy living with our children.

Whatever life one may be leading, one misses one's village very much.

In my view, our village is the best and the most hospitable place in the world.

Pathankot is not a very large city—but it is not so small a world either. It is situated on the common borders of Punjab, Himachal Pradesh and Jammu and Kashmir. My little village is located about fifteen kilometres from the Pathankot–Jalandhar Road. It is connected to other villages by an incomplete road because the Pathankot–Jalandhar railway line was laid near our village. This road, connecting three or four villages, does not cross the railway tracks. It has been left incomplete on both sides. The railway level crossing is unmanned. To prevent any motor cars from crossing the tracks and resulting in mishaps, five-foot-high iron posts have been fixed on both sides. People on cycles and scooters can cross the tracks. But a motor driver has to cover an extra distance of about five kilometres to reach the nearest railway crossing.

Of late, these complexities have doubled since a second track was laid down in the area.

The green hills of District Kangra in Himachal Pradesh look very pleasant from my village. You can see the tall palm trees on the eastern side of the village swaying in the sky. They look so graceful, like slender women dancing in single file.

At dawn, the sun, a lovely pop of red, rises from behind the mountain peaks, the beautiful spectacle beggaring all description.

Wait here until I come back after finishing the day's work, it seems to gently tell the palm trees being left behind in its ascent to meet the open sky.

No doubt, the sun returns to the earth as the evening sets in.

Like guardians of the village, large and shady mango trees stand on its outskirts. Nearby is a region with clayey soil. In the local dialect, we call it *shamas*. In this area lie storm drains and ponds. I still remember that we used to go to those drains and ponds to catch fish with a hook. We also went there to graze cattle. As we settled down at the edge of the pond to catch some rest, the silky blades of the green grass growing around soothed our tired feet.

I say with a very heavy heart, however, that everything has disappeared now.

All the families living here are refugees who were displaced from Pakistan years ago.

Before the Partition, Muslims of the Bharai community lived here. They were drum-beaters who performed during wrestling matches and other festive occasions to earn their living. As a result of the Partition, all those families migrated to Pakistan. Perhaps the village was named Chak Bharaiya after them.

The make up of the village is different now: about ten to twelve Rajput families, eight to ten water carrier families, five to six Ariyan families, some Brahmins, and a few barber and carpenter families. Besides these, no families belonging to any other religion or caste live in the village.

There is another important village near mine; About five kilometres away from us, Kaathgarh is situated on a small plateau on the Himachal border. On one side of the village flows a large serpentine drain. During the monsoons, this shamas assumes a very dangerous form. The water flows in full spate. Sometimes, this village is cut off from the neighbouring villages for a number of days. On the other side of the village flows the constantly hissing Beas.

Kaathgarh is famous for many reasons, especially an ancient Shiva temple that has a rock Shiva linga. The devotees believe that the linga appeared on its own. It is divided into two parts. The larger and higher part is called Lord Shiva, and the smaller and lower part is called Mother Parvati. As winter approaches, they start drawing closer to each other. And one day, the distance between them disappears completely. During the entire winter, they remain together in this warm embrace. The divine couple starts to draw apart as the summer season begins setting in over the months of February and March. At this time, a very large fair is held to mark the Shivaratri festival. People visit the village from all over the country to join in the celebrations.

Another legend of this area is connected with Lord Rama. It is believed that when his younger brothers Bharat and Shatrughan went to their maternal land, Kekahyee Pradesh (present-day Kashmir), they stopped on their way to worship this Shiva linga.

From a historical angle, this village is connected with Alexander the Great, the ruler of the ancient Greek kingdom of Macedon. It is said that this is the place where Alexander decided not to continue his military campaign against the Indian subcontinent. Because of the Shiva temple, the weapons of his army were rendered useless. The Beas caused terrible floods in the region. His army got tired and fed up. They refused to move forward.

At last, Alexander ordered his soldiers to retreat.

The Jalandhar–Pathankot line passes through the outskirts of our village. Now a double line has been built. When fast trains pass by, the houses tremble as if there is an earthquake. When a train passes by during the night, hissing and whistling, guests who are staying in the village for the first time get up with a start and call for help as they run out of the house. They feel as if the train has derailed from its tracks and is running towards them. They hesitate to visit the village again.

In the early days, the village boys rarely studied till the tenth class. Only one or two would sometimes pass the twelfth class. Most girls remained at home after passing the tenth or twelfth class. Rarely did a girl go to college. As soon as they turned eighteen, they were married off. The boys, after passing the tenth or twelfth, liked to be enrolled in the army. But now an awakening has dawned. People are serious about the education of their children.

Regardless, there is only one primary school in the village, where about eight to ten children study across various classes starting from the first to the fifth. There is only one teacher for all of them. She is the peon, teacher and headmistress of the school.

There is a Sarva Sanjhi Dehari Mata temple in the village. Incense is burnt in the temple every day. Lamps are lit. A *yagya* is also organized once a year. The elders play cards there. Whenever a village boy gets married and brings his bride home, the couple go to the temple the following day with the boy's cousins and their wives and circumambulate the periphery five times. The boy and his new bride lead the group while going round.

Long back, there was no temple in the village, so people collected money to build one. But that's it. There is no other place of worship—not one gurdwara, mosque or church. Perhaps that is why the village hasn't witnessed any caste-based or religious conflict thus far.

Yet there is some tension among the people. The government has built a community centre in the village, which also serves as the primary school. If needed, the villagers shelter their cattle in the temple campus during the monsoons or winter. There are one or two small local shops which offer only basic items such as tea, biscuits, sugar, salt, oil, etc. There are two wells in the village.

Now the Punjab government has provided houses with running water, accessed through taps and extracted by tube wells. Some people have installed water pumps in their houses.

There was no telephone in the village seven or eight years ago, but now five to seven houses have this facility. Mobile phones are also heard ringing in our area now. Only three or four houses in the village receive the newspaper. Rarely does anyone get an English newspaper. Cable TV has also reached our village. There is no young men's association or game society or literary forum in the village though. People here have no interest in literature, arts, etc. In my childhood, some of the villagers would get together and stage Ramlila, but this no longer happens.

Although many of the regions of the Punjab are backward, if I call my area the most backward, it would be no exaggeration.

In spite of all this, I don't know why, but my village keeps drawing me towards it.

Why do I feel the most peaceful only there?

What is this yearning for a visit that grips me every once in a while?

My village—it beckons my soul.

The most beautiful city in the country, Chandigarh, is where I have been living for nearly ten years. But Sector 17, Sukhna Lake, the Rock Garden, the Rose Garden, etc.,—all wonderful spots—never appear in my dreams. Rather, it's my village—friends, lanes, corners, trees, drains, ponds, dunes, wells—that subsume my subconscious.

Why have you forgotten us, dear friend? Why have you gone so far away? If only you could remember our shared times, I hear them echoing in unison.

I get up with a start and reality hits me like a splash of cold water—days past will not return.

There's hardly anything in my village that's worth bragging about. It has no historical importance. It has not given a big personality to the country. Still, I am very proud of my village.

It was my farmland that allowed me to stand on my two feet and meet the world with self-confidence. Every inch of the farm—every corner, every plant and every tree—was my fast friend. When we hurt ourselves cutting grass, we'd apply nothing but the mud of our land on the wound for alleviating the pain.

And now that we are living in Chandigarh, we no longer take care of the land like we used to.

A few years ago, we handed over our lands to relatives to farm. After some time, they gave up.

We then assigned the responsibility to someone else.

Those owning the adjoining pieces of land had started encroaching upon our land.

Our farmland had begun to be injured.

When we went to our fields, it seemed as if they were sad.

As if every tree and plant there had become motherless, holding us responsible for their bad state. Earlier, they seemed to be blooming with joy all the time. But now they look sick, and when a detractor of ours converted the adjacent land into a cremation ground, the fields, the trees and the plants became sadder still.

When we came to know from some people that some ill-intentioned persons were producing fake landowners in court and selling other peoples' lands, we were very worried. We feared being dispossessed of our land through such fake transactions.

Our land was two hundred and fifty kilometres away from Chandigarh.

Who would grapple with such disputes? This weighed heavily on our minds.

We made up our minds to sell the land so that it would prosper under the care of its new owner.

We found buyers for our land.

One day, they called us to come and collect the initial payment.

That we were going to give up our land caused us great sadness.

Bachno took it to heart.

Years ago, she had sold her gold bangles so that we could buy this land.

The life we had spent on our land flashed before our eyes like a film now. We could not bear to see our land crying in pain.

We gathered our courage and went to the village to sell our land.

The buyers paid me a part of the total price of the land, which was equal to the price of one acre. When I put that money in my small bag, I felt that one acre of land, with all its trees, plants, ponds and well had been squeezed to fit into the bag. When I lifted the bag, I felt I was carrying the weight of one acre of my land.

When we were returning to Chandigarh with the money, I felt we had sold not our land but our mother.

When we reached Chandigarh, we came to know that Bachno had been crying since the previous day.

When Bachno heard that the land had been sold, she shrieked and so did we.

When our daughters learnt about the sale of our land, they could not speak on the phone for grief. But another son had been found to take care of our Mother Earth. This gave us some solace.

All of us bowed our heads to our Mother Earth.

For the last ten years, we have been living in our small nest in Mohali.

My daily routine is to drop my grandsons and granddaughter off at the school bus stop in the morning and fetch them home in the afternoon.

Sometimes, I go to a shop to buy something for the house.

Sometimes, our daughters-in-law want their chunnis to be dyed. I put them in a paper bag and go to the dyer.

If Bachno tells me some shoes need repairing, I go to the cobbler.

Sometimes, I go to get our glasses repaired.

I keep myself busy.

I can never say no.

Every morning and evening, I visit the first floor of our house where we have built a small temple. I light a lamp and incense and say my prayers. In my small temple are kept pictures and idols symbolizing all the religions—Hinduism, Sikhism, Islam, Christianity—gurus, saints, pirs, faqirs, bhagats.

I have learnt the Hanuman Chalisa by heart. I regard Hanuman as the best and most powerful god, the reason being that he was a celibate.

Once, back when we were living in the village, I spent the entire night reading the Chalisa so that the moon would gain enough strength to free itself from the eclipse.

I had heard that the moon had borrowed some money from a demon but could not repay it, so in return, the demon was eating up the moon. When my children told me, 'Papa, it is nothing of that sort. The story of the moon taking a loan is a cock and bull story. It will make no difference to the moon if you go on reading the Hanuman Chalisa,' I replied that if there was no gain in reading it, then there was no loss either. Hanumanji can be remembered on this pretext.

If I am at home, no beggar leaves empty-handed from our place. If someone refuses to give alms to a beggar, I tell them:

Begging is just like dying
None should go begging
Dying is better than begging
This is our Guru's teaching.

But before him dies the one
Who says 'no' to a beggar.

Perhaps I know nothing about two things: lying and feeling tired.

I try my best to never tell a lie.

I advise others also to speak the truth.

I do not like to make false promises.

I always say, a miser is better than a so-called generous person as he is able to say no at once.

I am always full of energy and keep doing something or the other. This has become a habit. After finishing one task, I take up another.

This was the case in the village also.

In the compound of the house in Mohali, on a quarter of a small space, I have grown mangoes, guavas and lemons. There is a turmeric plant also. I have planted all kinds of flowering plants as well. Every year, I grow bottle gourd, pumpkin and sponge gourd.

Whenever I get the time, I tend the plants—watering, hoeing and pruning. I look after them as my children.

And after all these chores are done, I sit to read the newspaper.

In the afternoon, I take the children to the nearby park. Once home in the evening, I never forget to burn incense so that its fragrance spreads in every room, nook and corner of the house.

Then I light a lamp in the temple, collecting the ash from the previous lamp and smearing it on the foreheads of all the children.

This is my routine.

Every evening, all three of us—my two sons and I—sit together and drink our pegs.

When the children insist, I sing verses from 'Sassi Punnu', 'Puran Bhagat' or another folk tale to my liking.

I drink one or, maximum, two pegs—just small ones!

'I drink only to enjoy and feel high; it is not my weakness. So only this much is good enough for me,' I say when the children press me to take more.

When I eat, it is not to fill my belly to the rim.

'Bear this in mind, my sons, if you have an appetite for four chapattis, take only three, and if it is for three, take only two, and if it is for two, take one. And if you want to have only one chapatti, don't take anything. Otherwise, you will eat only to distend your belly,' I always advise my children.

I don't like lazy people at all.

I do not put off till tomorrow what I can do today.

I rest only when everything is done. I don't leave anything incomplete.

The last day for the payment of the electricity or water bill may be a week away, but I am always in a hurry to check such tasks off my list immediately.

Sometimes my children say, 'Papa, why do you get so worried about doing everything quickly?' But my argument always is that it is better to do something immediately than to defer it. Why wait till the eleventh hour? And if a bill is not paid timely, a late fee is charged.

Every month, I circle the important dates on the calendar—deadlines for bill payments, birthdays, etc.—so I do not forget them. I start reminding everyone of what is to be done three or four days in advance.

I remember, about twenty years ago, my elder son was struggling to settle down in Chandigarh and open his coaching centre. He had been married for the last two years.

My elder granddaughter had already arrived in the world.

In those days, Bachno and I lived in the village.

My struggle with life continued.

At the time, I had been sick for two to two and a half months.

I ran a temperature daily.

I was being treated by a village doctor.

The fever came down for some time.

But my routine continued to be hectic: I worked in the fields in the morning and hawked chappals in the evening.

A fortnight later, the fever became a permanent feature. I felt hot the whole day. Fatigue and weakness never evaded me.

And one day I collapsed in bed.

Bachno saw my yellow eyes and guessed that it was jaundice.

Worried, she suggested that I go to Chandigarh and consult a good doctor.

I reached the city the next evening.

As soon as I saw my elder son, I hugged him and cried.

'What is the matter, Papa?' he asked, stunned upon looking at my crestfallen face.

'I think my end is near now, my son. I may not live long. I thought I should meet my children for the last time,' I wailed loudly.

He took me to a doctor immediately.

The doctor performed several tests.

When he received the reports, he said that I had jaundice because of a liver infection. The chance of recovery was just one per cent. He told me that if I wished to live a little longer, I would have to give up drinking, at least for two years.

I immediately promised to lay off alcohol.

Soon, my treatment started.

From then on, a person like me, who earlier had a peg or two every day, did not even look at alcohol.

I did sit with my children at get-togethers but did not touch a single drop. Sometimes, on festive occasions, relatives insisted on my joining in but I resolutely denied.

Ultimately, I was victorious over jaundice, which could have proved fatal.

Two years later, I visited the same doctor. After conducting all the required tests, he smiled and said, 'Dear soldier, if you like, you can have a peg or two.'

Both my sons were very happy to have me back in their joyful company.

Now both our sons have relieved their mother and me of all our social and domestic responsibilities.

We simply enjoy the presence of our grandchildren.

It is a great pleasure spending time with them.

A keen mix of innocence and mischief, they keep us on our toes as we relive our own childhood through them. Their future will be bright, I am certain.

These days, whenever we visit our village, recollections from years ago stir in my mind as we drive through the neighborhoods where I once hawked chappals on a cycle and our sons sold vegetables. As I sit back in one of my children's big cars, protected from the heat and dust outside, mists and haze of the past pervade my mind during the ride. Flames flare up. Memories flash before my eyes like a film. The same village. The same people. The same lanes. The same roads. But not the same time. I imagine calling out to the people, *Do you recognize me? I am the same hawker. The one who used to cycle with one hand and sell chappals—a tunda. Those sitting with me are my children.*

Then I thank Him, who is high above. He saved me from becoming a beggar, and today my labour has borne fruit—I got the opportunity to lead a full and respectable life.

May pride never cloud my mind, my Master! I always pray to God with palms folded.

Epilogue

In 2005, I had some trouble passing urine. My younger son took me to the doctor's.

He examined me and ordered some tests.

The next day, I was taken to the doctor again.

My younger son brought along his elder brother as well.

'Dear friends, though it is disquieting, I have to tell you that your father has prostate cancer—that too of the last stage. Take him back home and look after him. He will survive a month or so longer—perhaps six months at the most. The treatment is very expensive, and it will be of no use. I will give some painkillers so that he does not feel great distress,' the doctor explained.

My sons were taken aback on hearing this, but they did not disclose the diagnosis to me. However,

I guessed reading their faces that everything was not all right. All the same, I kept the soldier within me alive. I did not let them know that I had an inkling that I was not well.

When I queried my sons on their discussion with the doctor, they attempted to mellow down the blow, telling me that my ailment was something ordinary, which would be cured very soon.

To dispel all doubts, they consulted another doctor. He too diagnosed me with cancer of the last stage.

Both my sons insisted that the doctor start my treatment.

Though he did not want to, he agreed.

The doctor prescribed some medicines and certain precautions, with a follow-up appointment a month later.

The brothers did not share my diagnosis with the family. They only said that I had an issue with my prostate, which is quite common among older men and was thus likely to cause our loved ones less worry.

My treatment began immediately.

At the next appointment, a month later, the doctor ordered some tests again post examining me.

When the reports came back, he was wonder-struck.

'Dear friends, in my long career, this is the first time I have seen a case where cancer at the last stage has returned to the first stage. It is a miracle. Your father is quite safe now. Of course, he will have to continue to take some medicines,' the doctor told both the brothers.

Very soon, everything returned to normal.

What the doctor had said proved right, and I was as fit as a horse, as they say in Punjabi. In fine fettle.

I resumed leading a normal life.

Rather enjoyed life.

My life once again seemed to be my own.

My elder son, Govardhan Gabbi, is a rising star among writers of Punjabi literature. Four of his books have been published so far.

Bachno and I, too, participate in literary meets along with him. When we are honoured there as important guests, we feel a great sense of pride.

Our happiness knows no bounds.

What's more, our younger son has become a successful doctor. When he takes us with him to social gatherings and we are introduced as the parents of the doctor, our chests swell with pride and joy.

Tears also wet our eyes, but these are tears of joy. We thank God for His blessings.

Our three daughters are happily married. Our three sons-in-law are decent people, who are successful professionally too.

Our eldest daughter has two sons. The middle daughter has a son and a daughter. The youngest one has a son.

Our youngest daughter, Sunita, is now living with her family in Canada.

We feel deeply gratified that our daughters are leading happy lives.

Both our daughters-in-law—the elder one is Raj Kumari and the younger, Shakha Rani—are very good-natured and well-mannered.

They look after us well.

The elder one manages her own private school.

The younger one teaches at a government school.

Govardhan has two children. The elder one is a daughter, Wamiqa, whom we fondly call Deebu. His son's name is Haardik, but we've always called him Munna.

Our younger son has two boys: the elder one, Garry, and the younger, Mugil.

My elder granddaughter Wamiqa is fast becoming another bright star of our family. When she was in the fifth class, she played a part in a TV serial. In the eighth class, she began to receive offers for acting roles.

All grown up, when she goes to various locations for shooting now, her grandmother and I accompany her sometimes. We are honoured greatly there also. When some well-known film star touches our feet to show respect, it feels strange.

We wonder if all this is really happening to us or to someone else.

These days, she is acting in Hindi and Punjabi films. She does theatre also.

Sometimes, I wonder, almost fearfully, why God is so kind to us. We thank Him for his great blessings.

The medicines I have been taking for my prostate cancer have impacted my kidneys.

Lately, there is swelling on my legs also.

I suffer from constipation too.

As a matter of fact, constipation has been with me since childhood.

My doctor son sometimes gives me purgatives.

Then loose motions trouble me for many days.

Sometimes, it is painful to urinate.

I also have stomach aches and other such ailments.

Contending with one issue or another, I feel unhappy most of the time.

My younger son has consulted other doctors. I have been diagnosed with a kidney problem.

A few days ago, I passed blood with urine.
My condition worsened.
The children admitted me to a private hospital.
The doctors said that I needed a blood transfusion.
Six bottles of blood were transfused.
I recovered in a week or so and am home now.
I wonder if the worst is over.

I remained quite well for a few days, but then the kidney problem returned. Three tubes have been inserted in my body—two in the flank and one in the bladder.

I do not like these tubes at all.

I feel very upset when I have to carry the bags attached to the tubes.

The children try to make me understand that the tubes are for my treatment. Regardless, I do not like it.

I put the tubes in a paper bag and try to hide them away from the gaze of others.

I can't sleep at night now.
Everyone in the family is worried about my health.
Bachno sits by my side throughout the night.

When the pains grow deeper, my children also wake up.

It's been a month or so since the tubes were put in. The doctors are removing them now.

I am greatly relieved.

Thank God!

Though my treatment isn't complete yet.

My younger son continues to get tests done.

My sugar, blood, cholesterol and urea reports show no abnormality. But I am still losing heart with every passing day.

With so much going on, I feel very weak.

I can't get up on my own now.

I have to go to the bathroom every half hour or so.

My younger son and elder grandson massage my legs daily.

My elder son also reassures me constantly.

My daughters-in-law spare no effort in looking after me.

One gives me soup to drink.

The other gives me juice.

Despite being reassured by my family, I am losing heart.

I am unhappy all the time.

'What is the matter, Papa? Your condition is improving, isn't it? Why are you despairing then?' my elder son asked me one day.

'There is nothing left, my son…There is no fun in living now. Is this even living? I am a bother to all of you—most of all, your mother. Now is the time for me to play with the children; instead they spend their days caring for me. I have suffered many hardships throughout my life, but I have never been dependent on anyone. Why is all this happening to me now? I must have done some bad deeds to be facing this misery. If this is called life, my son, let it be cursed a million times. I pray to God to call me back to Him. That will be the best for me.'

I began to cry.

'What are you saying, Papa? We have no control over illnesses. This body does get unwell sometimes. If you are ill, looking after you, getting you treated, is our duty. If you need our help to go to the bathroom, why feel ashamed of it? You are a soldier, Papa. A brave soldier. We are so proud of you. Don't lose heart. We are with you every step of the way and we need you very much. You have so much to do yet—you have to see your granddaughter become a heroine; two of her films are going to be released in a few days. Don't lose heart, you will get well soon.'

Both my sons try to encourage me.

'What sort of life can he have who is dependent on others!' I often say weeping.

I show courage for some time after listening to my children, but then my sickness overwhelms me again.

I am getting weaker day by day.

My younger daughter calls me every day from Canada.

She encourages me to show resilience.

Her goal is to keep my strength going.

My other daughters also call me regularly.

Relatives and neighbours often come over to enquire about my health.

My eyes turn wet when I see them.

'Why do you cry, Papa? We don't like this. You are a soldier, a brave person,' the children say.

'I do not want to cry, my children, but these wretched tears come out on their own.' I try to smile.

Bachno insists that I will recover.

'Dear one, I will not be fully well again. Even if I survive this bout of illness but stay troubled by one ailment or another, will it be a life worth living?'

I don't know what happened to me, but one day, I could not stop crying.

My elder son asked me why I was distressed.

I kept quiet.

He asked me again and again, but I avoided giving a reply.

'You have some burden on your mind, Papa. If you want to share some secret from your life, please tell me. I wonder if you have another Gabbi like me some place else whom you share your confidences with,' he jested to lighten the mood.

'Nothing of the sort. I am forced to see such days…Is this a quality life? No more, I say. Enough is enough!' I fell quiet again.

'Tell me, what is the matter? Did someone say something to upset you?'

'I passed stool and urine in my pyjama. Your mother was outside. Shabha had to clean everything. God had to show me such days,' I said, crying bitterly.

Today is 30 October 2012.

It is still morning.

My condition is deteriorating.

I am being taken to the hospital.

I am losing consciousness.

My entire body has been pierced with needles.

Many machines are examining my condition.

Many tubes and wires have been wrapped around me.

Doctors are coming to see me every few minutes.

Nurses are checking my blood pressure and heartbeat.

I am feeling sleepy.

Evening has set in.

'Are you all right, Papa?'

I recognize the voices of my family.

I can't move, but I can feel that my body lies punctured by needles and wrapped in bandages.

I open my eyes with great effort.

I indicate that I am feeling better.

I look at the sad faces all around.

Especially Bachno's countenance.

She sits by my side.

Her sweet words comfort me.

The others leave, promising to return later that night.

It is a little past 10 p.m.

My elder son, daughter-in-law and elder granddaughter have come to see me.

I can hear their voices.

They are enquiring about my health.

They are wishing me to get well soon.

They are asking me to rest.

Now then, they are leaving.

They hold my hand in theirs and say goodbye.

I too want to waive my hand, but a great weakness has set in.

I am unable to command my limbs.

No part of my body moves at my will anymore.

I open my eyes with great difficulty and try to bid them goodbye with just a look.

I see their eyes brimming with tears.

Mine are shutting down.

31 October 2012. It is 2.45 a.m.

I am feeling sleepy; I need to sleep a deep sleep.

All right, farewell, my dear friends.

Acknowledgements

I do not know what the literary genre of this book is. Is it a novel, biography, long story, poem or something else? For me, it is an account of the life led by my dear father, who was devoted to his family and society.

When his health began failing in his later years, Pappa ji started to jot down his memoirs at my insistence. He did so for almost four years. He would write a little about an incident before stopping to recount all that had happened. Then he would recall more bits and write further. In this way, he continued to record whatever he could piece together from his life of seventy-six years. And then on 31 October 2012, early in the morning, Pappa ji left us forever.

After that, I took up the task of turning his notes into a narrative, giving words to his sincere emotions. The resultant story is as pure as gold, but to turn it into a literary jewel, I might have added some impurity. All the characters in the book are real. Even their names have not been changed.

With the help of my life partner, Raj Kumari Kaushal, and other family members, who granted me time to work on the project with patient understanding, I was able to finish writing my father's life story. The original book was published in Punjabi as *Puran Katha* in 2015. I am grateful for their love and support.

Nearly a decade later, a fresh English translation by Dr Rajinder Singh has made my father's story accessible to new readers. Dr Singh has translated some of my other Punjabi writings too. I am grateful for all his efforts.

I must thank the extremely generous Vishal Bhardwaj for putting me in touch with the team at Om Books International, especially publisher Ajay Mago and chief editor Shantanu Ray Chaudhuri, who extended warm support throughout the process. My wonderful editor Soumya Duggal carefully refined the manuscript while retaining its original voice and idiom and my talented designer Sheena Agarwal designed a very striking cover.

Now that the book is out, I hope readers will embrace Pappa ji's innate optimism and indomitable spirit.